Diplomatic Dilemmas: State-sponsored Terrorism and International Relations

Copyright Page

TITLE: Diplomatic Dilemmas: State-sponsored Terrorism and International Relations

1ST Edition

Copyright @ 2023

Roberto M. Rodriguez. All rights reserved.

ISBN: 9798223659204

Diplomatic Dilemmas: State-Sponsored Terrorism and International Relations

By Roberto Miguel Rodriguez

Chapter 1: States Sponsoring Terrorism

Introduction to State-Sponsored Terrorism

State-sponsored terrorism is a complex and controversial topic that has garnered significant attention in recent years. This subchapter aims to provide an overview of the concept, examining its various dimensions and implications. Understanding state-sponsored terrorism is crucial, as it has a profound impact on international relations, security, and diplomacy.

States Sponsoring Terrorism:

The first section of this subchapter delves into the concept of states sponsoring terrorism. It explores the motivations behind state sponsorship, such as political objectives, ideological affiliations, or regional power struggles. It also highlights the ethical and legal dilemmas associated with state sponsorship and the challenges faced by the international community in addressing this issue.

State-Sponsored Terrorism in Specific Regions:

The subsequent sections of this subchapter focus on state-sponsored terrorism in different regions. It provides an in-depth analysis of state-sponsored terrorism in the Middle East, Asia, Africa, Latin America, and Europe. Each region has its unique dynamics, which contribute to the prevalence of state sponsorship. By examining these specific cases, readers can gain a deeper understanding of the causes, consequences, and implications of state-sponsored terrorism.

State-Sponsored Cyberterrorism:

With the rapid advancement sof technology, cyberterrorism has emerged as a significant concern. This section explores the growing trend of state-sponsored cyberterrorism, highlighting the potential consequences for national security, international relations, and global stability. It also discusses the role of intelligence agencies in detecting and countering cyber threats.

State-Sponsored Terrorism and Nuclear Proliferation:

This section examines the nexus between state-sponsored terrorism and nuclear proliferation. It explores how states can exploit terrorist organizations to further their nuclear ambitions, posing a grave threat to international security. The chapter discusses the challenges faced in preventing the proliferation of nuclear weapons and the role of international diplomacy in addressing this issue.

State-Sponsored Terrorism and Proxy Wars:

The next section analyzes the relationship between state-sponsored terrorism and proxy wars. It explores how states employ terrorist groups as proxies to achieve their strategic objectives, often leading to prolonged conflicts and regional instability. The section highlights the impact of proxy wars on international diplomacy and the challenges faced in resolving these conflicts.

State-Sponsored Terrorism and the Role of Intelligence Agencies:

The final section of this subchapter discusses the crucial role of intelligence agencies in countering state-sponsored terrorism. It explores the intelligence community's efforts in gathering information, analyzing threats, and conducting covert operations to disrupt state-sponsored terrorist activities. The section also highlights the ethical considerations and legal constraints faced by intelligence agencies in combating state-sponsored terrorism.

In conclusion, this subchapter provides a comprehensive overview of state-sponsored terrorism and its various dimensions. It addresses the concerns of scholars, academicians, and the general public, covering topics such as specific regions, cyberterrorism, nuclear proliferation, proxy wars, international diplomacy, and the role of intelligence agencies. By understanding the complexities and implications of state-sponsored terrorism, we can foster a more informed and effective approach to addressing this global challenge.

Historical Context of State-Sponsored Terrorism

State-sponsored terrorism has been a pervasive issue throughout history, and understanding its historical context is crucial to comprehending its evolution and impact in the present world. This subchapter delves into the historical origins, patterns, and consequences of state-sponsored terrorism, shedding light on its various forms and regions of influence.

States Sponsoring Terrorism:

The phenomenon of states sponsoring terrorism has deep historical roots, with numerous examples throughout history. From the Roman Empire's utilization of proxy groups to the state-sponsored terrorism during the French Revolution, this subchapter explores the historical antecedents of state involvement in terrorism.

State-sponsored terrorism in the Middle East:

The Middle East has long been a hotbed of state-sponsored terrorism. This subchapter examines the historical context of state sponsorship in the region, including the Iran-Iraq War, the Palestinian-Israeli conflict, and the rise of extremist groups like Hezbollah and Hamas.

State-sponsored terrorism in Asia:

Asia has also witnessed state-sponsored terrorism, with countries like North Korea and Pakistan drawing attention for their alleged support of terrorist organizations. This section explores historical cases, including the Tamil Tigers in Sri Lanka and the Japanese Red Army.

State-sponsored cyberterrorism:

Advancements in technology have given rise to a new form of state-sponsored terrorism – cyberterrorism. This subchapter examines the historical development of state-sponsored cyber attacks, including Stuxnet, the Sony hack, and the alleged involvement of state actors in hacking incidents.

State-sponsored terrorism in Africa, Latin America, Europe:

State-sponsored terrorism is not restricted to specific regions. This subchapter explores historical cases of state sponsorship in Africa, Latin America, and Europe, including the apartheid regime in South Africa, the Contras in Nicaragua, and terrorist incidents in Northern Ireland.

State-sponsored terrorism and nuclear proliferation:

Nuclear proliferation has been a grave concern, particularly when combined with state sponsorship of terrorism. This section explores historical cases such as Pakistan's alleged support for terrorist groups while developing its nuclear program.

State-sponsored terrorism and proxy wars:

State-sponsored terrorism often intertwines with proxy wars, where states employ terrorist groups as proxies to achieve their political objectives. This section delves into historical cases such as the Soviet-Afghan War and the Syrian conflict.

State-sponsored terrorism and international diplomacy:

The role of international diplomacy in addressing state-sponsored terrorism cannot be understated. This subchapter discusses historical diplomatic efforts, including sanctions, negotiations, and international agreements, aimed at curbing state sponsorship of terrorism.

State-sponsored terrorism and the role of intelligence agencies:

Intelligence agencies play a critical role in countering state-sponsored terrorism. This section explores historical instances where intelligence agencies have been involved in uncovering state sponsorship, such as the CIA's support for the Afghan Mujahideen during the Soviet-Afghan War.

By examining the historical context of state-sponsored terrorism, this subchapter aims to provide scholars, academicians, and the public with a comprehensive understanding of the origins, patterns, and consequences of this complex phenomenon. It offers valuable insights into the dynamics of state sponsorship in different regions, the evolving nature of terrorism, and the challenges faced by international diplomacy and intelligence agencies in combating this global threat.

Motivations behind State-Sponsored Terrorism

State-sponsored terrorism is a complex and disturbing phenomenon that has significant implications for international relations. Understanding the motivations behind such acts is crucial for scholars, academicians, and the public to grasp the dynamics of this distressing global issue. This subchapter delves into the motivations driving states to engage in the support and sponsorship of terrorism.

One of the primary motivations behind state-sponsored terrorism is the pursuit of political objectives. States sponsoring terrorism often aim to destabilize their adversaries, weaken their governments, or coerce them into compliance with their own political agendas. By utilizing terrorist groups as proxies, these states can maintain plausible deniability while achieving their desired outcomes. This motivation is particularly evident in regions such as the Middle East, Asia, Africa, Latin America, and Europe, where states have employed terrorist organizations to further their strategic interests.

Another motivation for state sponsorship of terrorism is the pursuit of regional dominance and influence. States sponsor terrorism to assert their power, expand their spheres of influence, and counter the influence of rival nations. In some cases, state-sponsored terrorism has been used as a tool to conduct proxy wars, allowing states to engage in conflict without direct military involvement. This has been witnessed in numerous conflicts, such as the proxy wars between Iran and Saudi Arabia in the Middle East or India and Pakistan in South Asia.

State-sponsored cyberterrorism has emerged as a new motivation in recent years. As technology continues to advance, states are increasingly employing cyberattacks as a means to achieve their political, economic, or military objectives. By utilizing hackers and cybercriminal networks, states can disrupt critical infrastructures, steal sensitive information, or sow chaos in rival nations. The role of intelligence agencies in such attacks cannot be ignored, as they play a significant part in planning, executing, and covering up state-sponsored cyberterrorism.

Furthermore, state-sponsored terrorism has become intertwined with nuclear proliferation concerns. Some states sponsor terrorism to acquire or maintain nuclear weapons, thereby enhancing their strategic position and deterring potential adversaries. The fear of nuclear terrorism has heightened the urgency for international diplomacy and cooperation in addressing this issue.

Understanding the motivations behind state-sponsored terrorism is essential for devising effective counterterrorism strategies and shaping international diplomacy. Scholars, academicians, and the public must engage in robust research and analysis to comprehend the intricacies of this phenomenon. By exploring the motivations behind state-sponsored terrorism, we can work towards fostering a safer and more peaceful global community.

Consequences of State-Sponsored Terrorism

State-sponsored terrorism is a complex and multifaceted phenomenon that has far-reaching consequences for both the sponsoring state and the international community as a whole. In this subchapter, we will delve into the various consequences of state-sponsored terrorism, highlighting its impacts on different regions, issues, and actors in the international arena.

One of the primary consequences of state-sponsored terrorism is the destabilization of regions, particularly in the Middle East and Asia. States sponsoring terrorism often provide financial, logistical, and ideological support to non-state actors, enabling them to carry out acts of violence and create chaos. This destabilization not only leads to loss of life and property but also undermines the social fabric of these regions, fueling sectarian tensions and perpetuating cycles of violence.

Furthermore, state-sponsored terrorism has extended its reach to the cyber realm, where states employ sophisticated techniques to carry out attacks on critical infrastructure, disrupt communication networks, and steal sensitive information. This form of terrorism poses a significant threat to national security and economic stability, requiring robust international cooperation to mitigate its consequences.

State-sponsored terrorism in Africa, Latin America, and Europe has also had profound implications. In Africa, countries such as Sudan and Libya have been known to support terrorist groups, exacerbating conflicts and impeding development efforts on the continent. Latin America has witnessed state-sponsored terrorism in the form of proxy wars and insurgencies, leading to widespread human rights abuses and political instability. In Europe, recent attacks have highlighted the increasing threat posed by state-sponsored terrorism and the urgent need for enhanced security measures and intelligence sharing.

The consequences of state-sponsored terrorism are not limited to specific regions. Nuclear proliferation has been a significant concern, with states using terrorist organizations as proxies to acquire or disseminate weapons of mass destruction. This dangerous nexus between state-sponsored terrorism and nuclear proliferation demands a comprehensive approach to non-proliferation efforts and international diplomacy.

Proxy wars, often fueled by states sponsoring terrorism, have devastating consequences for the countries involved and the wider international community. These conflicts prolong humanitarian crises, displace millions of people, and create fertile ground for extremism and radicalization. International diplomacy plays a crucial role in addressing these conflicts, urging states to cease support for terrorist groups and engage in peaceful negotiations.

Intelligence agencies also bear the brunt of state-sponsored terrorism. They must navigate the intricate web of state-sponsored terrorism networks, gather intelligence, and preempt attacks. Collaborative efforts among intelligence agencies are vital to effectively counter state-sponsored terrorism and mitigate its consequences.

In conclusion, state-sponsored terrorism has far-reaching consequences that impact various regions, issues, and actors in the international arena. From destabilizing regions and engaging in cyberterrorism to fueling nuclear proliferation and proxy wars, the consequences of state-sponsored terrorism demand a comprehensive and collaborative approach from scholars, academicians, the public, and relevant stakeholders to effectively counter this menace and preserve international peace and security.

Chapter 2: State-Sponsored Terrorism in the Middle East

Overview of State-Sponsored Terrorism in the Middle East

Introduction:

State-sponsored terrorism is a complex and significant issue that has major implications for international relations and global security. This subchapter aims to provide an overview of state-sponsored terrorism, with a focus on the Middle East region. It will examine the historical context, key actors, motivations, and consequences of state-sponsored terrorism in this volatile region.

Historical Context:

The Middle East has long been a hotbed of political and religious conflicts, making it a fertile ground for state-sponsored terrorism. From the Iranian Revolution in 1979 to the ongoing Syrian civil war, various states have utilized terrorism as a tool to achieve their political objectives. This subchapter will explore the roots of state-sponsored terrorism in the Middle East and its evolution over time.

Key Actors and Motivations:

Several Middle Eastern states have been accused of sponsoring terrorism, including Iran, Syria, Saudi Arabia, and Iraq under Saddam Hussein. These states often support non-state actors, such as Hezbollah and Hamas, providing them with financial, military, and ideological support. The motivations behind state-sponsored terrorism in the Middle East are diverse and include sectarian conflicts, regional power struggles, and anti-Western sentiments. This subchapter will delve into the specific motivations of different states and the groups they support.

Consequences:

State-sponsored terrorism in the Middle East has had far-reaching consequences for both regional and global security. It has fueled instability, perpetuated conflicts, and caused significant loss of life and displacement. Additionally, state-sponsored terrorism has led to the rise of extremist ideologies, contributed to the spread of radicalization, and strained diplomatic relations between states. This subchapter will examine these consequences and their impact on the region and beyond.

Conclusion:

Understanding the phenomenon of state-sponsored terrorism in the Middle East is crucial for scholars, academicians, and the general public. By exploring the historical context, key actors, motivations, and consequences, this subchapter provides a comprehensive overview of the topic. It highlights the complex interplay between state-sponsored terrorism, international relations, and global security. Furthermore, it sheds light on the role of intelligence agencies, the challenges faced in international diplomacy, and the connection between state-sponsored terrorism and nuclear proliferation or proxy wars. By examining state-sponsored terrorism in the Middle East, this subchapter contributes to a broader understanding of this pressing issue and offers insights for policymakers and practitioners in combating terrorism and promoting peace in the region.

Case Study: State-Sponsored Terrorism in Iran

Introduction

This subchapter delves into the case study of state-sponsored terrorism in Iran, examining the complex dynamics between the Iranian government, terrorism, and its impact on international relations. The aim is to provide scholars, academicians, and the public with a comprehensive understanding of the multifaceted nature of state-sponsored terrorism in the Middle East, the role of intelligence agencies, and its implications for international diplomacy.

State-Sponsored Terrorism in Iran: Historical Context

To comprehend Iran's involvement in state-sponsored terrorism, it is crucial to explore the historical context. The Iranian government has been accused of supporting various terrorist groups, including Hezbollah, Hamas, and the Houthi rebels. Iran's motivations for sponsoring terrorism often revolve around advancing its geopolitical objectives, exporting its revolutionary ideology, and countering perceived threats from regional rivals.

State-Sponsored Terrorism and International Relations

The impact of state-sponsored terrorism in Iran extends beyond the Middle East. The chapter investigates its implications for international relations, examining how Iran's support for terrorism has strained its relationships with Western powers and regional neighbors. It also explores the challenges faced by the international community in effectively addressing state-sponsored terrorism and the role of intelligence agencies in gathering evidence, surveillance, and counterterrorism efforts.

State-Sponsored Terrorism and Proxy Wars

Iran's involvement in proxy wars through state-sponsored terrorism is a critical aspect of its foreign policy. The subchapter analyzes Iran's use of proxy groups to advance its interests, such as its support for Hezbollah in Lebanon and the Houthis in Yemen. It examines the consequences of these proxy wars, including regional instability, humanitarian crises, and the impact on regional and global security.

State-Sponsored Terrorism and Nuclear Proliferation

One of the most significant concerns regarding Iran's state-sponsored terrorism activities is its nuclear program. The chapter investigates the relationship between state-sponsored terrorism and Iran's pursuit of nuclear weapons, highlighting the potential dangers posed by a nuclear-armed state involved in supporting terrorist organizations.

Conclusion

State-sponsored terrorism in Iran presents complex challenges for international relations, regional stability, and global security. This subchapter provides scholars, academicians, and the public with an insightful analysis of the historical context, motivations, and implications of Iran's involvement in state-sponsored terrorism. It emphasizes the need for robust international diplomacy, intelligence sharing, and collaborative efforts to address this pressing issue effectively. By understanding the intricate dynamics at play, policymakers and the public can work towards finding viable solutions to mitigate the impact of state-sponsored terrorism in Iran and its ripple effects across the globe.

Case Study: State-Sponsored Terrorism in Syria

Introduction:

The subchapter titled "Case Study: State-Sponsored Terrorism in Syria" delves into the complex and multifaceted issue of state-sponsored terrorism in the Middle East. Focusing specifically on Syria, this case study explores the significant implications of state sponsorship on international relations, diplomacy, intelligence agencies, and the overall global security landscape.

State-Sponsored Terrorism in Syria:

The Syrian conflict, which erupted in 2011, has been marred by state-sponsored terrorism, making it a critical case study for understanding the dynamics and consequences of this phenomenon. Scholars, academicians, and the public have a vested interest in comprehending the nuances of this conflict, given its implications for regional stability and global security.

States Sponsoring Terrorism:

The case study in Syria highlights the involvement of multiple state actors in supporting terrorist organizations. These states, driven by divergent interests, have provided financial, logistical, and military support to extremist groups, perpetuating violence and unrest in the region. The analysis of these state sponsors sheds light on their motivations, alliances, and the geopolitical implications of their actions.

State-Sponsored Terrorism in the Middle East, Asia, Africa, Latin America, and Europe:

The Syrian case study also provides an opportunity to examine the broader regional context. By comparing and contrasting state-sponsored terrorism in the Middle East with other regions such as Asia, Africa, Latin America, and Europe, scholars and academicians can identify common patterns, divergent strategies, and unique challenges faced by each region.

State-Sponsored Cyberterrorism:

In addition to traditional forms of state-sponsored terrorism, the case study explores the growing threat of state-sponsored cyberterrorism. Syria has been a hotbed for cyberattacks, raising concerns about the potential use of digital platforms to facilitate terrorism. Understanding the nexus between state sponsorship and cyberterrorism is crucial for developing effective countermeasures in the digital age.

State-Sponsored Terrorism and Nuclear Proliferation:

Examining the Syrian case study also provides insights into the interplay between state-sponsored terrorism and nuclear proliferation. The involvement of state sponsors in supporting extremist groups with access to weapons of mass destruction poses a significant threat to global security. This subchapter delves into the complexities surrounding nuclear proliferation and terrorist networks.

State-Sponsored Terrorism and Proxy Wars:

The Syrian conflict highlights the role of state-sponsored terrorism as a tool for proxy wars. Competing regional and global powers, seeking to advance their interests, have utilized extremist groups as proxies in the Syrian theater. This case study illuminates the interconnectedness between state sponsorship, proxy wars, and the prolongation of conflicts.

State-Sponsored Terrorism and International Diplomacy:

The subchapter explores the intricate relationship between state-sponsored terrorism and international diplomacy. The Syrian case study emphasizes the challenges faced by the international community in holding state sponsors accountable while maintaining diplomatic channels. Understanding this delicate balance is crucial for formulating effective strategies to combat state-sponsored terrorism.

State-Sponsored Terrorism and the Role of Intelligence Agencies:

Lastly, the Syrian case study sheds light on the pivotal role played by intelligence agencies in countering state-sponsored terrorism. Analyzing the intelligence efforts and failures in identifying and mitigating the impact of state sponsors provides valuable lessons for intelligence agencies worldwide.

Conclusion:

The case study of state-sponsored terrorism in Syria serves as a compelling illustration of the complex dynamics and far-reaching implications of this phenomenon. Scholars, academicians, and the public can gain a deeper understanding of the interplay between state sponsors, terrorism, international relations, and global security. This subchapter aims to contribute to the existing body of knowledge and foster meaningful discussions and debates in the fields of terrorism studies, international relations, diplomacy, and intelligence.

Case Study: State-Sponsored Terrorism in Saudi Arabia

Title: Case Study: State-Sponsored Terrorism in Saudi Arabia

Introduction:

The phenomenon of state-sponsored terrorism continues to be a pressing concern in the realm of international relations. This subchapter delves into a comprehensive case study on state-sponsored terrorism in Saudi Arabia, shedding light on its implications, causes, and potential solutions. By examining this specific case, we aim to provide scholars, academicians, and the public with a deeper understanding of the complex dynamics surrounding state-sponsored terrorism.

State-Sponsored Terrorism in Saudi Arabia:

Saudi Arabia, a prominent Middle Eastern nation, has been implicated in supporting and sponsoring terrorist activities in different parts of the world. This case study analyzes the historical context, motivations, and consequences of Saudi Arabia's involvement in state-sponsored terrorism. It explores the country's alleged connections with extremist groups and its utilization of financial resources to foster and propagate radical ideologies.

Impact on the Middle East and Asia:

The repercussions of state-sponsored terrorism in Saudi Arabia extend beyond its own borders. This section examines the destabilizing effects of Saudi Arabia's support for terrorism on both the Middle East and Asia. It highlights the rise of extremist groups, the exacerbation of sectarian tensions, and the consequent challenges faced by regional security apparatuses in combating terrorism in these regions.

The Role of Intelligence Agencies and International Diplomacy:

Understanding the nexus between state-sponsored terrorism, intelligence agencies, and international diplomacy is crucial. This subchapter explores the intricate relationship between Saudi Arabia's intelligence agencies and their involvement in supporting terrorist organizations. It also assesses the responses of the international community, analyzing the diplomatic efforts made to counter state-sponsored terrorism.

Addressing State-Sponsored Terrorism:

As scholars and academicians, it is imperative to identify potential solutions to counter state-sponsored terrorism. This subchapter evaluates various strategies that can be employed to mitigate the threats posed by Saudi Arabia's involvement in state-sponsored terrorism. It emphasizes the importance of international cooperation, intelligence sharing, targeted sanctions, and diplomatic pressure to curb such activities effectively.

Conclusion:

The case study on state-sponsored terrorism in Saudi Arabia provides valuable insights into the multifaceted dimensions of this pressing issue. By examining the impacts, causes, and potential solutions, this subchapter aims to contribute to the existing knowledge base on state-sponsored terrorism and foster informed discussions among scholars, academicians, and the public. It emphasizes the need for collective action and international cooperation to effectively combat state-sponsored terrorism and maintain global peace and security.

Comparison of State-Sponsored Terrorism in the Middle East

The Middle East has long been plagued by the phenomenon of state-sponsored terrorism, with various countries in the region utilizing non-state actors to further their strategic interests. This subchapter aims to provide an in-depth analysis and comparison of state-sponsored terrorism in the Middle East, shedding light on the different actors involved, their motivations, and the impact on regional and international security.

One of the key aspects of state-sponsored terrorism in the Middle East is the diverse range of actors involved. Countries such as Iran, Saudi Arabia, and Syria have been accused of supporting and financing terrorist groups, including Hezbollah, Hamas, and various factions in Iraq and Yemen. Each of these state sponsors has its own unique motivations, whether it is to counter regional rivals, promote their own ideological agenda, or destabilize neighboring countries. Understanding these motivations is crucial in formulating effective counter-terrorism strategies.

Another important aspect to consider is the impact of state-sponsored terrorism on regional stability and international relations. The Middle East has been marred by proxy wars and conflicts, fueled by state sponsors providing financial, military, and logistical support to their chosen non-state actors. This has led to the displacement of millions of people, the rise of extremist ideologies, and the exacerbation of sectarian tensions. Moreover, state-sponsored terrorism in the Middle East has also had international ramifications, with attacks targeting Western interests and the involvement of foreign powers in the region.

Additionally, this subchapter will also explore the role of intelligence agencies in state-sponsored terrorism. Intelligence agencies play a crucial role in gathering information, analyzing threats, and disrupting terrorist networks. Understanding the capabilities and limitations of intelligence agencies in combating state-sponsored terrorism is vital for scholars and policymakers alike.

Finally, the subchapter will touch upon the issue of nuclear proliferation and its connection to state-sponsored terrorism. The fear of terrorist groups acquiring weapons of mass destruction has intensified concerns over state sponsors providing support to these groups. The case of Iran's nuclear program and its alleged links to Hezbollah is a prime example of this complex nexus.

In conclusion, this subchapter provides a comprehensive overview of state-sponsored terrorism in the Middle East. By comparing the different state sponsors, their motivations, and the impact on regional and international security, scholars, academicians, and the public can gain a deeper understanding of this pressing issue. Additionally, exploring the role of intelligence agencies, nuclear proliferation, and the connections to proxy wars and international diplomacy will further enrich the analysis.

Chapter 3: State-Sponsored Terrorism in Asia

Overview of State-Sponsored Terrorism in Asia

State-sponsored terrorism is a complex phenomenon that has significant implications for international relations and global security. This subchapter provides an overview of state-sponsored terrorism in Asia, focusing on the various actors involved, their motivations, and the consequences for regional stability.

Asia has been a hotbed of state-sponsored terrorism, with several countries in the region engaging in this form of covert warfare to further their political agendas. States sponsoring terrorism in Asia include Iran, North Korea, Pakistan, and to some extent, China and Russia. These states often provide financial, logistical, and ideological support to non-state actors, such as terrorist organizations, insurgent groups, and separatist movements.

State-sponsored terrorism in Asia is primarily driven by political motivations. States may sponsor terrorism to achieve strategic objectives, such as destabilizing rival states, asserting influence in a particular region, or advancing their ideological goals. For instance, Iran has been known to support Hezbollah in Lebanon and Hamas in Palestine as a means to challenge Israeli and Western interests in the Middle East.

The consequences of state-sponsored terrorism in Asia are far-reaching. It exacerbates existing conflicts, prolongs regional instability, hampers economic development, and threatens the lives of innocent civilians. Furthermore, state-sponsored terrorism often spills over national borders, creating transnational security challenges. The rise of state-sponsored cyberterrorism poses an additional threat, as states employ sophisticated hacking techniques to target critical infrastructure, disrupt communication networks, and steal sensitive information.

Efforts to counter state-sponsored terrorism in Asia require a multi-dimensional approach. International cooperation, intelligence sharing, and diplomatic negotiations are crucial in addressing the root causes of this phenomenon. Strengthening the capacity of intelligence agencies and law enforcement organizations is essential to detect and disrupt terrorist networks.

Moreover, addressing the underlying political and socio-economic grievances that fuel state-sponsored terrorism is of paramount importance. This requires engaging in meaningful dialogue, promoting good governance, and fostering economic development to provide vulnerable populations with alternative paths to pursue their aspirations.

In conclusion, state-sponsored terrorism in Asia is a pressing issue that demands the attention of scholars, academicians, policymakers, and the general public. By understanding the dynamics, motivations, and consequences of state-sponsored terrorism, we can work towards developing effective strategies to mitigate this threat and promote peace and stability in the region.

Case Study: State-Sponsored Terrorism in North Korea

Introduction:

State-sponsored terrorism is a complex and controversial issue that has significant implications for international relations and global security. This subchapter explores the case study of state sponsored terrorism in North Korea, shedding light on the tactics employed by the regime and the consequences for regional stability. By examining this specific instance, we can gain valuable insights into the broader phenomenon of state-sponsored terrorism.

Background:

North Korea, under the leadership of the Kim dynasty, has long been accused of engaging in state-sponsored terrorism. The regime has a history of exporting violence and instability beyond its borders, utilizing various means such as assassinations, cyberattacks, and proxy wars. This case study provides a comprehensive analysis of these activities, shedding light on their motivations, methods, and consequences.

Methods and Tactics:

North Korea's state-sponsored terrorism activities encompass a wide range of methods. These include the infamous assassination of Kim Jong-nam, the half-brother of North Korean leader Kim Jong-un, using a deadly nerve agent in a Malaysian airport. The regime has also been implicated in cyberattacks, such as the Sony Pictures hack, which revealed its ability to inflict significant damage on foreign entities. Additionally, North Korea has supported proxy wars, providing military aid and training to groups such as Hezbollah and Hamas.

Regional and Global Implications:

The state-sponsored terrorism activities of North Korea have far-reaching implications for regional stability and global security. By engaging in acts of terrorism, the regime seeks to assert its dominance, intimidate its adversaries, and secure its survival. However, these actions pose a significant threat to neighboring countries and undermine international peace and stability. The international community must recognize and address this threat to prevent further escalation and potential armed conflicts.

Conclusion:

The case study of state-sponsored terrorism in North Korea highlights the complex nature of this phenomenon and its multifaceted impact on international relations. As scholars and academicians, it is crucial to understand the motivations, methods, and consequences of state-sponsored terrorism to develop effective strategies for countering this threat. By examining the North Korean case, we can gain valuable insights into the broader dynamics of state-sponsored terrorism in Asia and beyond. Only through comprehensive research, international cooperation, and diplomatic efforts can we hope to mitigate the risks posed by state-sponsored terrorism and uphold global peace and security.

Case Study: State-Sponsored Terrorism in Pakistan

Introduction:

State-sponsored terrorism is an alarming global phenomenon with severe implications for international security and diplomacy. This subchapter examines a compelling case study: state-sponsored terrorism in Pakistan. By exploring the historical context, motives, and consequences of this phenomenon, we aim to shed light on the intricate dynamics of state-sponsored terrorism and its impact on international relations.

Historical Context:

Pakistan has long been plagued by state-sponsored terrorism, with its intelligence agencies allegedly providing support to various extremist groups. This support has been primarily motivated by regional power dynamics, religious ideologies, and geopolitical interests. The case study delves into the inception and evolution of state-sponsored terrorism in Pakistan, tracing its roots back to the Soviet-Afghan War in the 1980s and subsequent proxy wars in the region.

Motives and Consequences:

The subchapter analyzes the motives behind Pakistan's involvement in state-sponsored terrorism, including the desire to exert influence in neighboring countries, counter Indian influence, and secure strategic assets. It also explores the consequences of this policy, such as the rise of extremist ideologies, increased violence, and regional instability. The impact of state-sponsored terrorism on Pakistan's international reputation, foreign policy, and diplomatic relations is also examined.

International Diplomacy and Intelligence Agencies:

The subchapter highlights the role of international diplomacy in addressing state-sponsored terrorism in Pakistan. It discusses the challenges faced by the international community in holding state sponsors accountable and the need for collective action to combat this menace. Additionally, it examines the role of intelligence agencies in facilitating or countering state-sponsored terrorism, emphasizing the importance of intelligence cooperation and information sharing.

Implications for Global Security:

State-sponsored terrorism in Pakistan has broader implications for global security, nuclear proliferation, and the rise of cyberterrorism. The subchapter explores the connections between state-sponsored terrorism and nuclear proliferation, discussing the risks posed by terrorist groups gaining access to nuclear weapons or materials. It also examines the emerging threat of state-sponsored cyberterrorism and its potential to disrupt critical infrastructure and destabilize nations.

Conclusion:

The case study of state-sponsored terrorism in Pakistan provides valuable insights into the complex interplay between state actors, extremist groups, and international relations. By understanding the motives, consequences, and implications of state-sponsored terrorism, scholars, academicians, and the public can foster informed discussions and propose effective strategies to counter this grave threat. The subchapter encourages further research and dialogue on state-sponsored terrorism, emphasizing the need for international cooperation, intelligence sharing, and diplomatic efforts to mitigate its devastating impact on global security.

Case Study: State-Sponsored Terrorism in India

India has long been a victim of state-sponsored terrorism, a phenomenon that has had significant implications for international relations. This case study sheds light on the various dimensions of state-sponsored terrorism in India, exploring its roots, consequences, and the role of intelligence agencies in combating this menace.

State-sponsored terrorism in India primarily originates from neighboring countries, particularly Pakistan and Bangladesh. These states have been accused of providing safe havens, training, and financial support to terrorist groups operating against India. The most notorious of these groups is Lashkar-e-Taiba, responsible for the 2008 Mumbai attacks that claimed the lives of several innocent civilians. State-sponsored terrorism in India not only poses a threat to its national security but also fuels tensions and disrupts regional stability.

The Middle East has been a hotbed for state-sponsored terrorism, with many states in the region supporting extremist groups. These groups often find refuge in India, using it as a base to plan and execute terrorist activities. Similarly, state-sponsored terrorism in Asia has been a cause of concern, with countries like China and North Korea allegedly backing terrorist outfits targeting India.

In recent years, state-sponsored cyberterrorism has emerged as a significant threat. India has faced numerous cyber-attacks originating from state-sponsored actors, aiming to disrupt critical infrastructure, steal sensitive information, and spread propaganda. The rise of cyberterrorism has necessitated a robust response from Indian intelligence agencies to counter these threats effectively.

State-sponsored terrorism is not limited to the Middle East and Asia. It has also plagued Africa, Latin America, Europe, and other regions. The global nature of this issue underscores the need for international cooperation and diplomacy to address this menace collectively. State-sponsored terrorism often goes hand in hand with nuclear proliferation and proxy wars, further complicating the geopolitical landscape.

International diplomacy plays a crucial role in tackling state-sponsored terrorism. India has sought the support of the international community, highlighting the grave consequences of state-sponsored terrorism and urging for coordinated action against its sponsors. Intelligence agencies play a vital role in identifying and neutralizing state-sponsored terrorist networks, gathering evidence to expose their links to state actors.

In conclusion, state-sponsored terrorism in India is a complex issue with far-reaching implications. Scholars, academicians, and the public must understand the various dimensions of this problem to devise effective strategies to counter it. International cooperation, intelligence sharing, and diplomatic efforts are essential to combat state-sponsored terrorism and maintain global peace and security.

Comparison of State-Sponsored Terrorism in Asia

State-sponsored terrorism is a complex phenomenon that has significant implications for international relations. This subchapter aims to provide an in-depth analysis and comparison of state-sponsored terrorism in Asia, shedding light on the unique characteristics and challenges presented by this region. It is intended for scholars, academicians, and the general public interested in understanding the dynamics of state-sponsored terrorism and its impact on global security.

When examining state-sponsored terrorism in Asia, it is essential to consider the diverse range of actors involved and their motivations. Several countries in the region have been accused of supporting terrorist groups to further their political, ideological, or strategic interests. For instance, Pakistan has long been accused of providing support to various militant groups operating in Afghanistan and India. Similarly, North Korea has been implicated in state-sponsored acts of terrorism, such as the bombing of Korean Air Flight 858.

One key aspect of state-sponsored terrorism in Asia is its connection to proxy wars and international diplomacy. Many states in the region have sought to advance their interests by supporting non-state actors in neighboring countries. For example, Iran has been accused of backing Shia militias in Iraq, while Saudi Arabia has been implicated in supporting Sunni extremist groups. These proxy wars not only fuel regional conflicts but also complicate international diplomatic efforts to resolve them.

Another significant concern in Asia is state-sponsored cyberterrorism. Countries like China and North Korea have been accused of conducting cyber-attacks against foreign governments, organizations, and individuals. These attacks pose unique challenges, as they are difficult to trace and can have far-reaching consequences, including economic disruption and the compromise of sensitive information.

Furthermore, the issue of state-sponsored terrorism and nuclear proliferation is of utmost importance in Asia. States like Iran and North Korea, which have been accused of supporting terrorist groups, are also pursuing nuclear weapons programs. The intersection of these two threats raises serious concerns about regional and global security.

Understanding state-sponsored terrorism in Asia requires a comprehensive analysis of the role played by intelligence agencies. These agencies are often responsible for planning, coordinating, and executing acts of terrorism on behalf of states. Examining the dynamics between intelligence agencies and state-sponsored terrorism can provide valuable insights into the motivation, tactics, and strategies employed.

In conclusion, state-sponsored terrorism in Asia is a multifaceted issue with significant implications for international relations. This subchapter has provided an overview of the unique characteristics and challenges associated with state-sponsored terrorism in the region. By understanding these dynamics, scholars, academicians, and the public can contribute to the development of effective strategies to counter this threat and promote global security.

Chapter 4: State-Sponsored Cyberterrorism

Introduction to State-Sponsored Cyberterrorism

In the digital age, the threat of state-sponsored cyberterrorism has emerged as a significant concern in international relations. This subchapter of "Diplomatic Dilemmas: State-Sponsored Terrorism and International Relations" aims to provide an introduction to this growing menace, addressing audiences ranging from scholars and academicians to the general public.

State-sponsored terrorism refers to the support, encouragement, or involvement of a government in terrorist activities. While traditional forms of terrorism, such as bombings and kidnappings, have long been studied, cyberterrorism has gained prominence due to its potential to inflict widespread damage on critical infrastructure, economies, and national security.

The Middle East has witnessed numerous instances of state-sponsored terrorism, with countries like Iran and Syria often accused of supporting terrorist organizations. Asia, too, has seen its share of state-sponsored terrorism, with North Korea being a prime example, known for its cyber capabilities and involvement in cyber warfare.

However, the focus of this subchapter lies in exploring state-sponsored cyberterrorism, which transcends geographical boundaries and has the potential to disrupt nations worldwide. State-sponsored cyberterrorism involves the use of digital tools and techniques to attack the critical infrastructure, military systems, and economic interests of other countries, often with the aim of furthering political or strategic objectives.

Africa, Latin America, Europe, and other regions have experienced varying degrees of state-sponsored cyberterrorism, with attackers exploiting vulnerabilities in computer systems and networks to gain unauthorized access or disrupt services. The increasing interconnectedness of the world has made it easier for state-sponsored cyberterrorists to operate across borders and launch attacks remotely, making attribution and response challenging.

This subchapter will also explore the relationship between state-sponsored terrorism and nuclear proliferation, proxy wars, international diplomacy, and the role of intelligence agencies. It will delve into the complex dynamics between states sponsoring terrorism and their relationships with other nations, examining how these activities shape global politics and impact international security.

By understanding the nature and implications of state-sponsored cyberterrorism, scholars, academicians, and the public can gain insights into the evolving challenges faced by governments, policymakers, and intelligence agencies. This knowledge is crucial in developing effective strategies to counter and mitigate the threats posed by state-sponsored cyberterrorism, fostering international cooperation, and safeguarding critical infrastructure in the digital age.

Case Study: State-Sponsored Cyberterrorism in China

Introduction:

State-sponsored cyberterrorism has become a significant concern in today's interconnected world. This subchapter delves into a detailed case study on China, exploring its involvement in state-sponsored cyberterrorism activities. By examining China's cyber capabilities, motives, and targets, we aim to shed light on the complex dynamics of state-sponsored cyberterrorism and its implications for international relations.

China's Cyber Capabilities:

China has emerged as a global cybersecurity powerhouse, boasting formidable capabilities in both offensive and defensive cyber operations. Its vast pool of talented hackers, state-of-the-art technology, and extensive internet infrastructure make it a force to reckon with in cyberspace. China's cyber units, such as the PLA's Unit 61398, are believed to engage in state-sponsored cyber espionage and cyberattacks on foreign entities.

Motives for State-Sponsored Cyberterrorism:

China's motivations for engaging in state-sponsored cyberterrorism are multifaceted. Firstly, it seeks to gain a strategic advantage by stealing intellectual property, trade secrets, and sensitive military information from other nations. This contributes to its economic and military growth. Additionally, cyberattacks can serve as a tool for suppressing political dissidence, monitoring activists, and controlling information flow within its borders.

Targets of Cyberattacks:

China's cyber operations have targeted various countries and sectors. State-sponsored attacks have focused on governments, multinational corporations, defense contractors, and critical infrastructure. Notable incidents include the hacking of the U.S. Office of Personnel Management, the theft of intellectual property from numerous countries, and cyber espionage against neighboring Asian nations. These attacks highlight China's intent to gather intelligence, exert influence, and gain a competitive edge on the global stage.

Implications for International Relations:

China's state-sponsored cyberterrorism activities pose significant challenges to international relations. They erode trust between nations, threaten national security, and disrupt global economic stability. The theft of intellectual property and trade secrets can harm the competitiveness of affected countries, hampering innovation and economic growth. Furthermore, cyberattacks targeting critical infrastructure can lead to severe consequences, including power outages and compromised national security.

Conclusion:

Understanding the complexities of state-sponsored cyberterrorism is crucial for scholars, academicians, and the public. This case study on China's involvement in state-sponsored cyberterrorism provides valuable insights into the motives, targets, and implications of such activities. It underscores the need for international cooperation, robust cybersecurity measures, and diplomatic efforts to address the growing threat of state-sponsored cyberterrorism. By examining this specific case, we can better comprehend the broader challenges posed by state-sponsored terrorism and its intersection with international relations, intelligence agencies, and global security.

Case Study: State-Sponsored Cyberterrorism in Russia

Title: Case Study: State-Sponsored Cyberterrorism in Russia

Introduction:

In this subchapter, we delve into a compelling case study that explores the emergence and implications of state-sponsored cyberterrorism in Russia. By analyzing the tactics, motives, and consequences of this cyber threat, we aim to shed light on the evolving nature of state-sponsored terrorism in the context of international relations. This case study not only serves as a cautionary tale but also provides valuable insights into the complex relationship between state-sponsored terrorism, international diplomacy, and the role of intelligence agencies.

The Russian Cyber Threat:

Russia has emerged as a formidable player in the realm of cyberterrorism. With its advanced cyber capabilities, the Russian government has been accused of orchestrating cyber-attacks against various countries, organizations, and individuals. These attacks range from interference in foreign elections to the targeting of critical infrastructures, such as energy and transportation systems, and even alleged involvement in global ransomware campaigns.

Motives and Objectives:

Understanding the motives behind Russia's state-sponsored cyberterrorism is crucial in comprehending its larger objectives. While geopolitical aspirations, information warfare, and economic espionage are often cited as major motivators, it is essential to recognize that Russia's cyber activities are part of a broader strategy to assert influence, destabilize adversaries, and promote its national interests.

Implications for International Relations:

The rise of state-sponsored cyberterrorism poses significant challenges to international relations. The interconnectedness of cyberspace allows state-sponsored actors to operate anonymously, blurring the lines between state and non-state actors. This subchapter explores the ramifications of such attacks on global stability, national security, and the delicate balance of power among nations.

Role of Intelligence Agencies and International Diplomacy:

To effectively counter state-sponsored cyberterrorism, intelligence agencies play a pivotal role in collecting and analyzing cyber threat intelligence. Collaboration and information sharing among nations become paramount in enhancing cybersecurity and mitigating the risks associated with state-sponsored cyberterrorism. Moreover, international diplomacy plays a crucial role in establishing norms, rules, and regulations governing cyberspace, as well as fostering cooperation to address cyber threats collectively.

Conclusion:

This case study on state-sponsored cyberterrorism in Russia highlights the urgent need for scholars, academicians, and the public to comprehend the evolving landscape of state-sponsored terrorism. By examining the Russian cyber threat, we gain valuable insights into the motivations, implications, and countermeasures associated with state-sponsored cyberterrorism. Ultimately, addressing this complex issue necessitates a multi-faceted approach that combines intelligence efforts, international cooperation, and robust diplomatic strategies.

Case Study: State-Sponsored Cyberterrorism in the United States

Title: Case Study: State-Sponsored Cyberterrorism in the United States

Introduction:

The rise of technology and its integration into our daily lives has brought about new challenges in the realm of international relations. This subchapter delves into a specific case study that explores the growing threat of state-sponsored cyberterrorism in the United States. By examining the motives, methods, and consequences of such attacks, we aim to shed light on the complexities surrounding this form of terrorism and its implications for global security.

The Evolving Landscape of State-Sponsored Terrorism:

State-sponsored terrorism has long been a concern in international relations. This subchapter discusses the various regions of the world where state-sponsored terrorism is prevalent, such as the Middle East,

Asia, Africa, Latin America, and Europe. It delves into the unique characteristics and motivations of each region, highlighting the role of intelligence agencies and their impact on international diplomacy.

The Emergence of State-Sponsored Cyberterrorism:

With the increasing reliance on digital systems, state-sponsored cyberterrorism has emerged as a powerful tool for both state and non-state actors. This subchapter explores the concept of state-sponsored cyberterrorism, examining its definition, manifestations, and the challenges it poses to national security. It analyzes the potential effects of cyberattacks on critical infrastructure, economy, and public trust in government institutions.

Case Study: State-Sponsored Cyberterrorism in the United States:

Drawing upon real-world events, this subchapter presents a case study focusing on the United States. It analyzes notable cyberattacks, such as the Stuxnet worm, attributed to state-sponsored actors. By dissecting the motives and methods employed, this case study offers valuable insights into the strategies employed by states engaged in cyberterrorism and the potential consequences for national and international security.

Implications for Global Security and Diplomacy:

State-sponsored cyberterrorism has implications beyond the immediate targets of the attacks. This subchapter explores the impact on global security, including the nexus between state-sponsored terrorism and nuclear proliferation, as well as proxy wars. It also investigates the role of intelligence agencies in countering cyber threats and the importance of international cooperation in addressing this evolving challenge.

Conclusion:

This subchapter provides a comprehensive examination of state-sponsored cyberterrorism in the United States, presenting it as a case study within the broader context of state-sponsored terrorism worldwide. By understanding the motives, methods, and consequences of these attacks, scholars, academicians, and the public can gain valuable insights into the role of intelligence agencies, international diplomacy, and the need for enhanced cybersecurity measures to counter this growing threat.

Consequences and Countermeasures of State-Sponsored Cyberterrorism

In today's interconnected world, the threat of state-sponsored cyberterrorism has become a major concern for scholars, academicians, and the public alike. This subchapter aims to explore the consequences of state-sponsored cyberterrorism and discuss potential countermeasures to mitigate this growing threat.

States sponsoring terrorism are increasingly turning to cyber attacks as a means to achieve their objectives. The consequences of such attacks can be devastating, not only for the targeted state but also for the international community as a whole. State-sponsored cyberterrorism poses a significant risk to critical infrastructure, national security, and the economy. Disruption of power grids, financial systems, or communication networks can lead to chaos and instability. Moreover, cyber attacks can compromise sensitive government information, military secrets, and the privacy of individuals, resulting in long-term damage to a nation's security and reputation.

In the Middle East, state-sponsored terrorism has been a persistent issue, and the use of cyber tactics has further exacerbated this problem. Governments in the region have been known to employ cyber attacks to target their adversaries, disrupt social media platforms, or spread propaganda. Similarly, in Asia, state-sponsored cyberterrorism has been on the rise, particularly with nations engaged in territorial disputes or political conflicts. Africa, Latin America, and Europe have also experienced their fair share of state-sponsored cyber attacks, often aimed at influencing elections, destabilizing governments, or promoting extremist ideologies.

To effectively counter state-sponsored cyberterrorism, a comprehensive approach is required. International cooperation, information sharing, and the establishment of norms and regulations are crucial. States must work together to develop robust cybersecurity frameworks, enhance their capabilities, and increase resilience against cyber threats. Collaboration between intelligence agencies and law enforcement agencies is essential for detecting and attributing cyber attacks, ultimately holding the responsible state sponsors accountable.

Moreover, addressing the root causes of state-sponsored terrorism is paramount. Efforts should be made to engage in dialogue and diplomacy to resolve political conflicts and grievances that fuel terrorism. Additionally, the international community must actively work towards preventing the proliferation of nuclear weapons, as the nexus between state-sponsored terrorism and nuclear proliferation poses an imminent threat to global security.

In conclusion, state-sponsored cyberterrorism has far-reaching consequences, impacting not only the targeted states but also the stability of the international system. Scholars, academicians, and the public must be aware of the evolving nature of this threat and the need for comprehensive countermeasures. By fostering international cooperation, enhancing cybersecurity capabilities, and addressing the root causes of state-sponsored terrorism, we can strive towards a safer and more secure world.

Chapter 5: State-Sponsored Terrorism in Africa

Introduction:

State-sponsored terrorism is a grave threat to international peace and security, and Africa has not been immune to its pernicious effects. This subchapter aims to provide an overview of state-sponsored terrorism in Africa, shedding light on its causes, manifestations, and implications. By understanding this phenomenon, scholars, academicians, and the public can gain valuable insights into the complex dynamics of state-sponsored terrorism and its impact on international relations.

Causes and Motivations:

State-sponsored terrorism in Africa can be attributed to various factors, including political instability, ethnic tensions, economic disparities, and ideological extremism. State sponsors often exploit these vulnerabilities to advance their geopolitical interests, maintain regional dominance, or manipulate domestic politics. Additionally, external actors seeking to gain influence in the region may provide financial, logistical, or ideological support to terrorist groups, exacerbating the problem.

Manifestations and Regional Hotspots:

Africa has witnessed several instances of state-sponsored terrorism, with certain regions emerging as hotspots. One such area is the Horn of Africa, where state sponsors have supported militant groups like Al-Shabaab, destabilizing Somalia and posing a threat to the wider region. In West Africa, state-sponsored terrorism has manifested through the activities of Boko Haram and the Islamic State in the

Greater Sahara (ISGS), causing widespread violence, displacement, and humanitarian crises. Other regions, such as the Sahel and North Africa, have also experienced the impact of state sponsorship, with groups like Al-Qaeda in the Islamic Maghreb (AQIM) and Ansar al-Sharia posing security challenges.

Implications for International Relations:

State-sponsored terrorism in Africa has far-reaching implications for international relations. It undermines regional stability, hampers economic development, and exacerbates existing conflicts. Moreover, it poses a transnational threat, as terrorist groups often collaborate across borders, leading to the potential spillover of violence into neighboring countries and beyond. The international community, including the United Nations and regional organizations like the African Union, must address this issue collectively through diplomatic efforts, intelligence sharing, and targeted sanctions.

Conclusion:

Understanding the overview of state-sponsored terrorism in Africa is crucial for scholars, academicians, and the public alike. By comprehending the causes, manifestations, and implications of this phenomenon, stakeholders can work towards developing effective counterterrorism strategies, promoting regional cooperation, and enhancing international diplomacy. Only through concerted efforts can the scourge of state-sponsored terrorism be effectively combated, leading to a more peaceful and secure Africa, and a world free from the menace of terrorism.

Case Study: State-Sponsored Terrorism in Nigeria

Title: Case Study: State-Sponsored Terrorism in Nigeria

Introduction:

State-sponsored terrorism is a complex phenomenon that poses significant challenges to the international community. This subchapter explores a case study of state-sponsored terrorism in Nigeria, shedding light on the dynamics, implications, and the role of international diplomacy in combating this menace. By analyzing the specific context in Nigeria, we aim to provide insights applicable to the broader study of state-sponsored terrorism worldwide.

Background:

Nigeria, a country located in West Africa, has been plagued by terrorism for decades. In recent years, the rise of Boko Haram, an extremist group notorious for its brutal tactics and ideological agenda, has exposed the involvement of state actors in supporting and enabling terrorism within the country. This case study aims to delve into the various dimensions of state-sponsored terrorism in Nigeria, shedding light on its causes, consequences, and potential solutions.

State-Sponsored Terrorism and Proxy Wars:

The involvement of state actors in supporting terrorist organizations often manifests through the use of proxy wars. In Nigeria, certain factions within the government have been accused of providing financial, logistical, and ideological support to groups like Boko Haram. This subchapter explores the intricate web of alliances and motivations that drive state-sponsored terrorism in Nigeria.

State-Sponsored Terrorism and International Diplomacy:

The international community plays a crucial role in addressing state-sponsored terrorism. This section examines the diplomatic challenges faced by countries dealing with Nigeria's state-sponsored terrorism, emphasizing the importance of international cooperation, intelligence sharing, and coordinated efforts in countering this threat. It also highlights the role of regional organizations such as the African

Union and the Economic Community of West African States (ECOWAS) in fostering collaboration and promoting stability.

Implications and the Role of Intelligence Agencies:

State-sponsored terrorism in Nigeria has far-reaching implications, including the destabilization of the region, human rights abuses, and economic repercussions. This subchapter explores the role of intelligence agencies in gathering information, analyzing threats, and formulating effective counter-terrorism strategies. It also highlights the need for intelligence cooperation between states and the challenges associated with balancing national security interests and human rights concerns.

Conclusion:

This case study on state-sponsored terrorism in Nigeria provides valuable insights into the broader discourse on terrorism, international relations, and diplomacy. By examining the specific context of Nigeria, scholars, academicians, and the general public can gain a deeper understanding of the complexities surrounding state-sponsored terrorism. Ultimately, this knowledge can contribute to the development of more effective strategies to combat this global threat and promote peace and stability worldwide.

Case Study: State-Sponsored Terrorism in Somalia

Title: Case Study: State-Sponsored Terrorism in Somalia

Introduction:

In this subchapter, we delve into a detailed case study of state-sponsored terrorism in Somalia. As one of the most volatile regions in Africa, Somalia has been marred by years of political instability, which has enabled state-sponsored terrorism to flourish.

This case study highlights the dynamics between state actors, terrorism, and international relations, shedding light on the complex challenges faced in addressing this issue.

Understanding the Context:

Somalia, located in the Horn of Africa, has long been plagued by civil war, weak governance, and a lack of socio-economic development. These factors have created an environment conducive to the rise of non-state actors and state-sponsored terrorism. The involvement of external powers, such as neighboring countries and global actors, further complicates the situation.

State-Sponsored Terrorism in Somalia:

This section explores how various state actors have supported terrorist organizations within Somali territory. It examines the motivations behind such sponsorship, whether for political, ideological, or strategic reasons. The case study also analyzes the tactics employed by these groups and their impact on regional stability.

Consequences for the Region:

State-sponsored terrorism in Somalia has far-reaching consequences for the wider African continent. This section highlights the spillover effects of terrorism, including increased refugee flows, arms trafficking, and the destabilization of neighboring countries. It emphasizes the urgent need for regional and international cooperation to combat this threat effectively.

International Response:

Analyzing the international response to state-sponsored terrorism in Somalia, this section explores the role of diplomacy, intelligence agencies, and international organizations. It examines the effectiveness of existing counterterrorism strategies, the challenges faced by stakeholders, and the importance of intelligence sharing and collaboration.

Lessons Learned and Recommendations:

Drawing insights from the Somali case study, this section provides valuable lessons for scholars, academicians, and policymakers. It emphasizes the need for a comprehensive approach that combines security measures with efforts to address the root causes of terrorism, such as poverty, political marginalization, and weak governance. Recommendations for improved international cooperation, intelligence sharing, and capacity-building are also included.

Conclusion:

State-sponsored terrorism in Somalia serves as a stark reminder of the complex challenges faced by the international community in combating this global menace. By understanding the dynamics of state sponsorship, its consequences, and the role of various actors, scholars, academicians, and the public can contribute to informed debates and the development of effective strategies to counter this threat.

Case Study: State-Sponsored Terrorism in Sudan

Introduction:

In this subchapter, we will delve into a case study on state-sponsored terrorism in Sudan. Sudan, situated in Northeast Africa, has been plagued by the scourge of state-sponsored terrorism for decades. This case study aims to provide an in-depth analysis of the factors that have contributed to Sudan's involvement in such activities, the consequences it has faced, and the implications for international relations.

Background:

Sudan's history with state-sponsored terrorism can be traced back to the 1980s when it became a safe haven for various extremist groups, including Al-Qaeda under the leadership of Osama bin Laden. The Sudanese government, then led by President Omar al-Bashir, openly supported and provided sanctuary to these groups, allowing them to operate freely within its borders.

Factors:

Several factors have contributed to Sudan's involvement in state-sponsored terrorism. Firstly, the country's geographical location, bordering countries like Egypt, Libya, and Chad, has made it an attractive base for extremist groups seeking strategic advantages. Additionally, political instability, economic struggles, and a weak central government have provided fertile ground for terrorist organizations to flourish.

Consequences:

Sudan's sponsorship of terrorism has had severe consequences both domestically and internationally. Domestically, it has fueled internal conflicts and insurgencies, leading to widespread violence and displacement of civilians. Internationally, Sudan's actions have strained its diplomatic relations with other countries, particularly the United States, which has labeled Sudan as a state sponsor of terrorism.

Implications:

The implications of Sudan's state-sponsored terrorism go beyond its borders. It has contributed to the destabilization of the entire region, fostering an environment conducive to terrorist activities. Furthermore, Sudan's involvement in terrorism has led to increased international scrutiny and pressure, resulting in sanctions and diplomatic isolation.

Conclusion:

The case study of state-sponsored terrorism in Sudan serves as a stark reminder of the complexities surrounding this issue. It highlights the role of geographical factors, political instability, and weak governance in fostering an environment conducive to terrorism. Moreover, it underscores the far-reaching consequences and implications of state-sponsored terrorism, not only for the sponsoring state but also for international peace and security.

This case study provides valuable insights for scholars, academicians, and the public interested in understanding the dynamics of state-sponsored terrorism. It also caters to various niches, such as state-sponsored terrorism in Africa, international diplomacy, and the role of intelligence agencies. By examining the Sudanese case, we gain a deeper understanding of the challenges faced by states sponsoring terrorism and the urgent need for international cooperation to combat this global menace.

Comparison of State-Sponsored Terrorism in Africa

State-sponsored terrorism has become a prominent issue in today's international relations, with various regions across the globe experiencing its devastating consequences. One such region is Africa, where state-sponsored terrorism has taken on unique characteristics and poses distinct challenges. This subchapter aims to provide an in-depth analysis and comparison of state-sponsored terrorism in Africa, shedding light on its causes, manifestations, and implications.

Africa has witnessed the rise of state-sponsored terrorism primarily due to political instability, weak governance, and ethnic conflicts. Several states in Africa have resorted to supporting terrorist groups as a means to further their geopolitical interests, suppress dissent, or destabilize rival governments. While the motivations behind state sponsorship may vary, the consequences are often severe and far-reaching.

In comparing state-sponsored terrorism in Africa with other regions, such as the Middle East, Asia, Latin America, and Europe, it becomes evident that Africa faces a unique set of challenges. Unlike the Middle East, where state-sponsored terrorism is often driven by religious or sectarian differences, Africa's state-sponsored terrorism is fueled by ethnic rivalries and territorial disputes. Similarly, in Asia, state-sponsored terrorism is often linked to separatist movements or insurgencies, whereas in Africa, it is often associated with rebel groups seeking political power.

Furthermore, state-sponsored cyberterrorism has emerged as a growing concern in Africa. While the focus has primarily been on state-sponsored cyber activities in developed countries, African states have also been involved in cyber espionage, hacking, and disinformation campaigns. This form of state-sponsored terrorism has the potential to disrupt critical infrastructure, compromise national security, and undermine public trust.

Another critical aspect to consider is the nexus between state-sponsored terrorism and nuclear proliferation. While Africa may not have seen as many instances of nuclear proliferation as other regions, the potential for terrorist groups to acquire or exploit nuclear materials cannot be overlooked. The international community must remain vigilant in preventing such scenarios and ensuring nuclear security measures are in place.

The role of intelligence agencies in combating state-sponsored terrorism cannot be underestimated. Effective intelligence sharing and cooperation between African nations, as well as with international partners, are crucial in identifying and neutralizing state-sponsored terrorist networks. Additionally, international diplomacy plays a vital role in addressing the root causes of state-sponsored terrorism in Africa, such as poverty, political marginalization, and ethnic tensions.

In conclusion, state-sponsored terrorism in Africa presents unique challenges and requires a comprehensive understanding of its causes and manifestations. By comparing it with state-sponsored terrorism in other regions, scholars, academicians, and the public can gain valuable insights into the complexities of this issue. Addressing state-sponsored terrorism in Africa necessitates a multi-faceted approach that involves intelligence agencies, international diplomacy, and cooperation among African nations and their global partners. Only through concerted efforts can we hope to mitigate the devastating impact of state-sponsored terrorism in Africa and promote peace and stability in the region.

Chapter 6: State-Sponsored Terrorism in Latin America

Overview of State-Sponsored Terrorism in Latin America

Introduction:

State-sponsored terrorism is a complex and controversial issue that has significant implications for international relations and global security. This subchapter provides an overview of state-sponsored terrorism in Latin America, highlighting its historical roots, key actors, and the impact on regional stability. By examining this specific region, we can gain valuable insights into the broader dynamics of state-sponsored terrorism and its various manifestations worldwide.

Historical Context:

Latin America has been a hotbed of state-sponsored terrorism for several decades, with various countries utilizing terrorist tactics to advance their political agendas. During the Cold War, both the United States and the Soviet Union engaged in covert operations and supported proxy groups to further their interests in the region. This period witnessed the rise of leftist guerrilla movements, such as the Revolutionary Armed Forces of Colombia (FARC) and the Shining Path in Peru, which received support from external sponsors.

Key Actors:

Several Latin American countries have been implicated in supporting terrorism either directly or indirectly. Cuba, for instance, has a long history of providing safe havens and training camps for leftist guerrilla groups throughout the region. Venezuela, under the leadership of Hugo Chávez and Nicolás Maduro, has been accused of supporting groups like the National Liberation Army (ELN) and providing assistance to Colombian drug cartels.

Impact on Regional Stability:

State-sponsored terrorism in Latin America has had a profound impact on regional stability. It has contributed to the proliferation of illegal activities, including drug trafficking and organized crime, which further undermine governance and economic development. Additionally, the presence of terrorist groups has led to widespread violence, human rights abuses, and displacement of populations, exacerbating social and political tensions in affected countries.

International Response:

The international community has recognized the threat posed by state-sponsored terrorism in Latin America and has taken steps to address it. Regional organizations such as the Organization of American States (OAS) and the Union of South American Nations (UNASUR) have condemned these activities and have called for increased cooperation to combat terrorism. However, the effectiveness of these measures remains limited, primarily due to the complex geopolitical dynamics and the involvement of powerful external actors.

Conclusion:

State-sponsored terrorism in Latin America represents a significant challenge to regional stability and international security. It is crucial for scholars, academicians, and the public to understand the historical context, key actors, and the impact of these activities. By analyzing state-sponsored terrorism in Latin America, we can draw important lessons and insights that can inform our understanding of this phenomenon in other regions, such as the Middle East, Asia, Africa, and Europe. Furthermore, this knowledge can contribute to the development of effective strategies to counter state-sponsored terrorism, enhance international diplomacy, and strengthen the role of intelligence agencies in preventing and mitigating this global threat.

Case Study: State-Sponsored Terrorism in Cuba

Introduction

The subchapter titled "Case Study: State-Sponsored Terrorism in Cuba" delves into the specific instance of state-sponsored terrorism in the Latin American region, focusing on Cuba. This case study offers a unique perspective on the complexities of state-sponsored terrorism and its implications for international relations. Scholars, academicians, and the public interested in understanding the multifaceted nature of state-sponsored terrorism and its impact on global security will find this subchapter particularly enlightening.

Background

Cuba has long been associated with state-sponsored terrorism, with its government allegedly supporting and harboring various extremist groups. This subchapter examines the historical context and ideological motivations that have driven Cuba's involvement in state-sponsored terrorism. It explores the country's historical ties with other state sponsors of terrorism, such as the Soviet Union during the Cold War era, and the subsequent shift in alliances following the dissolution of the Soviet Union.

State-Sponsored Terrorism in Cuba: Tactics and Objectives

The subchapter delves into the specific tactics employed by Cuba in its state-sponsored terrorism activities, including the provision of training, funding, and safe havens to terrorist organizations. It also explores the objectives behind Cuba's support for terrorism, such as advancing its revolutionary ideology, countering perceived threats to its regime, and exerting influence in the region.

International Response and Diplomatic Dilemmas

This subchapter analyzes the international response to Cuba's state-sponsored terrorism, focusing on the diplomatic dilemmas faced by the international community in addressing this issue. It examines the challenges of holding state sponsors accountable, the role of intelligence agencies in uncovering evidence, and the effectiveness of diplomatic efforts in curbing Cuba's support for terrorism.

Implications for Global Security

By examining the case of state-sponsored terrorism in Cuba, this subchapter offers valuable insights into the broader implications for global security. It explores the interconnectedness between state-sponsored terrorism and proxy wars, nuclear proliferation, and cyberterrorism. It also highlights the role of intelligence agencies in combating state-sponsored terrorism and the need for enhanced international cooperation to address this complex challenge.

Conclusion

The case study on state-sponsored terrorism in Cuba provides a comprehensive analysis of Cuba's involvement in supporting and harboring terrorist organizations. Addressed to scholars, academicians, and the public interested in various aspects of state-sponsored terrorism, this subchapter sheds light on the complex dynamics, diplomatic dilemmas, and implications for global security. It serves as a valuable resource for understanding the multifaceted nature of state-sponsored terrorism and its impact on international relations.

Case Study: State-Sponsored Terrorism in Venezuela

Title: Case Study: State-Sponsored Terrorism in Venezuela

Introduction:

The subchapter "Case Study: State-Sponsored Terrorism in Venezuela" sheds light on the alarming trend of state-sponsored terrorism in Latin America. Focusing specifically on Venezuela, this case study explores the complex dynamics between state actors, terrorism, and international relations. By analyzing the country's political landscape, its association with state-sponsored terrorism, and the implications for regional and global security, this chapter aims to provide scholars, academicians, and the public with a comprehensive understanding of this critical issue.

Understanding State-Sponsored Terrorism in Venezuela:

Venezuela, a country plagued by political instability and economic challenges, has become a fertile ground for state-sponsored terrorism. The subchapter delves into the factors contributing to this phenomenon, such as the authoritarian regime's support for non-state actors and their violent activities, including drug trafficking, arms smuggling, and money laundering. By exploring the historical context and the rise of state-sponsored terrorism in Venezuela, we gain valuable insights into its regional and global implications.

Implications for Regional and Global Security:

The case study highlights the potential consequences of state-sponsored terrorism in Venezuela for neighboring countries and the international community. It examines how terrorism, fueled by state actors, can undermine regional stability, exacerbate existing conflicts, and breed transnational criminal networks. Furthermore, the subchapter explores the implications of Venezuela's state-sponsored terrorism for the various regions addressed in this book, including the Middle East, Asia, Africa, Europe, and the role of intelligence agencies.

The Role of International Diplomacy:

In addressing the challenges posed by state-sponsored terrorism in Venezuela, the subchapter emphasizes the crucial role of international diplomacy. It explores the possibilities for diplomatic interventions, regional cooperation, and multilateral efforts aimed at curbing state sponsorship of terrorism. By assessing the effectiveness of diplomatic initiatives, scholars, academicians, and the public can gain insights into potential strategies to combat state-sponsored terrorism in Venezuela and beyond.

Conclusion:

This subchapter serves as a comprehensive analysis of the case study on state-sponsored terrorism in Venezuela, offering valuable insights into the complex dynamics between state actors, terrorism, and international relations. By addressing the concerns of various niches, including states sponsoring terrorism, regional dynamics, cyberterrorism, nuclear proliferation, and intelligence agencies' role, this chapter provides a holistic understanding of the far-reaching consequences of state-sponsored terrorism. It aims to foster informed discussions and guide policymakers, scholars, and academicians in developing effective strategies to counter this growing threat to global security.

Case Study: State-Sponsored Terrorism in Colombia

In this subchapter, we delve into a compelling case study of state-sponsored terrorism in Colombia, shedding light on the intricate dynamics and consequences of such actions. Through an in-depth analysis, we aim to provide scholars, academicians, and the public with a comprehensive understanding of the complexities surrounding state-sponsored terrorism in Latin America.

Colombia has long been plagued by internal conflicts, with various armed groups fighting for political control and territorial dominance.

Among these groups, the Revolutionary Armed Forces of Colombia (FARC) has emerged as a significant player, engaging in acts of terrorism to advance its political agenda. However, what makes the Colombian case unique is the involvement of state actors in supporting and sponsoring these acts of terrorism.

State-sponsored terrorism in Colombia is characterized by a complex web of relationships between the government, armed groups, and paramilitary forces. The Colombian government, in its efforts to combat these insurgencies, has been accused of employing tactics that blur the line between counter-terrorism and state-sponsored terrorism. This includes allegations of providing financial support, intelligence, and even weapons to paramilitary groups, who then carry out acts of terrorism on behalf of the state.

The consequences of state-sponsored terrorism in Colombia are far-reaching. The civilian population suffers the most, with countless innocent lives being lost or disrupted by acts of violence. Moreover, the destabilization caused by these actions hampers the country's socio-economic development and undermines the trust between the government and its citizens.

Examining this case study is crucial for understanding the wider implications of state-sponsored terrorism globally. By exploring the intricate connections between state actors, armed groups, and the consequences for civilian populations, we can draw important lessons for states sponsoring terrorism, state-sponsored terrorism in other regions such as the Middle East, Asia, Africa, and Europe, and the role of intelligence agencies in tackling this issue.

This analysis also sheds light on the diplomatic dilemmas faced by the international community in responding to state-sponsored terrorism. It highlights the challenges of balancing national security concerns with ethical considerations and the need for effective international cooperation to address this complex issue.

In conclusion, the case study of state-sponsored terrorism in Colombia offers valuable insights into the multifaceted nature of this phenomenon. By understanding the dynamics, consequences, and diplomatic dilemmas associated with state-sponsored terrorism, scholars, academicians, and the public can contribute to developing effective strategies for combating this global challenge.

Comparison of State-Sponsored Terrorism in Latin America

The phenomenon of state-sponsored terrorism has been a prominent feature in international relations, with various regions of the world experiencing its effects differently. In this subchapter, we will focus on the specific case of Latin America and compare it to other regions that have grappled with state-sponsored terrorism.

Latin America has witnessed a complex history of state-sponsored terrorism, characterized by a unique set of circumstances and dynamics. Unlike the Middle East or Asia, where state-sponsored terrorism has often been fueled by religious or ethnic tensions, Latin America has been driven by ideological conflicts and political struggles. During the Cold War, the United States and the Soviet Union played a significant role in fueling state-sponsored terrorism in the region, with each superpower supporting opposing factions to advance their own geopolitical interests.

Unlike Europe, where state-sponsored terrorism has been relatively limited in recent decades, Latin America continues to grapple with its legacy. Guerrilla movements, such as the Revolutionary Armed Forces of Colombia (FARC) and the Shining Path in Peru, have engaged in acts of violence against the state, often with funding and support from external actors. These groups have pursued radical ideologies and sought to overthrow established governments, leading to prolonged conflicts and widespread human rights abuses.

Furthermore, Latin America has also faced the challenge of state-sponsored cyberterrorism. Both state and non-state actors have utilized cyberattacks to advance their political agendas and undermine their adversaries. For instance, countries like Brazil and Mexico have experienced cyberattacks on their critical infrastructure, highlighting the vulnerability of the region to this emerging form of terrorism.

In contrast to Africa, where state-sponsored terrorism has been driven primarily by ethnic and religious tensions, Latin America's conflicts have been more ideologically and politically motivated. However, it is important to note that the lines between state and non-state actors in Latin America can often blur, with intelligence agencies and military forces playing a significant role in supporting or combating terrorist groups.

The comparison of state-sponsored terrorism in Latin America with other regions highlights the diverse factors and motivations driving this phenomenon. Understanding these nuances is crucial for scholars, academicians, and the general public, as it allows for a comprehensive analysis of state-sponsored terrorism and its implications for international relations, nuclear proliferation, proxy wars, and the role of intelligence agencies. By examining the specificities of state-sponsored terrorism in Latin America, we can gain valuable insights into the broader dynamics of this global phenomenon and explore potential strategies for its prevention and resolution.

Chapter 7: State-Sponsored Terrorism in Europe

Overview of State-Sponsored Terrorism in Europe

State-sponsored terrorism is a complex and multifaceted phenomenon that has had a significant impact on international relations. This subchapter aims to provide an overview of state-sponsored terrorism specifically in Europe, exploring its causes, manifestations, and consequences. It is intended for scholars, academicians, and the public interested in understanding the dynamics of state-sponsored terrorism and its implications for global security.

Europe has witnessed various forms of state-sponsored terrorism throughout history, with different states employing terrorist tactics to pursue their political objectives. The origins of state-sponsored terrorism in Europe can be traced back to the Cold War era, when both Western and Eastern bloc countries utilized terrorism as a means to exert influence and undermine their adversaries. Examples include the activities of the Red Brigades in Italy, the Baader-Meinhof Group in Germany, and the Provisional Irish Republican Army (IRA) in the United Kingdom.

State-sponsored terrorism in Europe has evolved in recent years, taking on new dimensions and posing new challenges. One notable trend is the emergence of state-sponsored cyberterrorism, where states employ cyber warfare techniques to target critical infrastructure and disrupt the functioning of their adversaries. This form of terrorism has the potential to cause widespread damage and disruption, making it a significant concern for European countries and the international community.

Furthermore, the rise of extremist ideologies and the radicalization of individuals have led to an increase in the number of European citizens joining terrorist organizations abroad. Some European states have been accused of turning a blind eye to these activities, raising questions about their role in indirectly supporting terrorism.

State-sponsored terrorism in Europe also intersects with other global challenges, such as nuclear proliferation and proxy wars. Some states have provided support to non-state actors in their pursuit of nuclear weapons, while others have used terrorist groups as proxies in regional conflicts. These actions have far-reaching implications for regional stability and international diplomacy.

Understanding the dynamics of state-sponsored terrorism in Europe requires a comprehensive analysis of the role of intelligence agencies. Intelligence gathering and sharing play a crucial role in combating terrorism, and effective cooperation among European intelligence agencies is essential to address this threat collectively.

In conclusion, state-sponsored terrorism in Europe is a complex and evolving phenomenon that requires careful analysis. This subchapter provides an overview of the various dimensions of state-sponsored terrorism in Europe, including its historical roots, emerging trends, and intersections with other global challenges. By shedding light on these issues, it aims to contribute to the understanding of state-sponsored terrorism and its implications for international relations and global security.

Case Study: State-Sponsored Terrorism in Russia

Title: Case Study: State-Sponsored Terrorism in Russia

Introduction:

The subchapter "Case Study: State-Sponsored Terrorism in Russia" delves into the complex and multifaceted issue of state-sponsored terrorism, focusing specifically on its manifestation in Russia. This case study aims to shed light on the tactics employed by the Russian government, its motivations, and the implications for international relations and global security. By examining this specific case, scholars, academicians, and the general public can gain a deeper understanding of the broader phenomenon of state-sponsored terrorism and its various implications.

State-Sponsored Terrorism in Russia:

Russia has a long history of state-sponsored terrorism, utilizing both traditional and unconventional methods to achieve its objectives. This case study explores the Russian government's involvement in various acts of terrorism, including assassinations, bombings, and cyberattacks. The analysis includes an examination of its support for separatist movements, proxy wars, and the alleged use of intelligence agencies to carry out covert operations.

Implications for International Relations:

The subchapter highlights the profound impact of state-sponsored terrorism on international relations. It emphasizes the destabilizing effect of Russia's actions on neighboring countries, particularly those in Eastern Europe and Central Asia. Moreover, the study underscores the challenges posed by state-sponsored terrorism to global security, including the potential for nuclear proliferation and the exacerbation of proxy conflicts.

Role of Intelligence Agencies:

A key focus of this case study is the role of intelligence agencies in state-sponsored terrorism. It examines how Russian intelligence agencies have been allegedly involved in orchestrating and executing terrorist attacks, while operating with a high degree of deniability. The analysis also considers the intelligence community's evolving role in countering state-sponsored terrorism and the implications for international diplomacy.

Conclusion:

The case study on state-sponsored terrorism in Russia provides a comprehensive analysis of the tactics, motivations, and implications of this phenomenon. By examining this specific case, scholars, academicians, and the public can gain insights into the broader issue of state-sponsored terrorism and its impact on international relations. It emphasizes the need for robust international cooperation, intelligence sharing, and diplomatic efforts to effectively address the challenges posed by state-sponsored terrorism. Overall, this subchapter contributes to a deeper understanding of the complexities surrounding state-sponsored terrorism and its implications for global security.

Case Study: State-Sponsored Terrorism in Turkey

Introduction:

State-sponsored terrorism is a complex and multifaceted phenomenon that has significant implications for international relations and global security. This subchapter delves into the specific case of state-sponsored terrorism in Turkey, shedding light on the motives, methods, and consequences of this alarming trend. By examining the Turkish context, we aim to provide scholars, academicians, and the general public with a comprehensive understanding of the dynamics surrounding state-sponsored terrorism, its regional and global impact, and the role of various actors involved.

Background:

Turkey, a country located at the crossroads of Europe and Asia, has been grappling with the menace of state-sponsored terrorism for several decades. The Turkish government has faced challenges from various terrorist organizations, both domestic and international, which have received support and backing from state actors. This chapter explores the motives behind state sponsorship of terrorism in Turkey, the methods employed by these state actors, and their consequences for national and international security.

State-Sponsored Terrorism in Turkey:

The subchapter analyzes the involvement of different states in sponsoring terrorism within the Turkish context. It examines how these state actors exploit ethnic, religious, and political fault lines within Turkey to further their own geopolitical interests. The subchapter also explores the relationship between state-sponsored terrorism and proxy wars, shedding light on the role of foreign intelligence agencies in fueling and perpetuating violence.

Consequences and Implications:

By examining the case of state-sponsored terrorism in Turkey, we can better understand the wider implications for international diplomacy, intelligence gathering, and counterterrorism efforts. This subchapter highlights the challenges faced by the Turkish government and the international community in combating state-sponsored terrorism. It also explores the impact of state-sponsored terrorism on regional stability, nuclear proliferation, and cyberterrorism, emphasizing the need for coordinated international action.

Conclusion:

State-sponsored terrorism in Turkey represents a significant diplomatic dilemma, with far-reaching consequences for global security. By studying this case, scholars, academicians, and the public can gain insight into the broader issues surrounding state-sponsored terrorism, including its impact on different regions, the role of intelligence agencies, and the challenges faced by international diplomacy. This subchapter aims to contribute to the ongoing discourse on state-sponsored terrorism and its implications for international relations, urging stakeholders to address this pressing issue through informed action and collaboration.

Case Study: State-Sponsored Terrorism in France

Introduction:

State-sponsored terrorism is a complex and sensitive issue that has far-reaching implications for international relations. This subchapter delves into a case study on state-sponsored terrorism in France, highlighting the various dimensions and consequences of this phenomenon. By analyzing the French experience, we can gain valuable insights into the broader challenges posed by state-sponsored terrorism worldwide.

Background:

France has faced numerous incidents of state-sponsored terrorism, with various actors employing different tactics. These incidents have had a significant impact not only on France but also on the global security landscape. By examining these cases, we can better understand the motivations behind state-sponsored terrorism and its implications for international diplomacy, intelligence agencies, and proxy wars.

State-Sponsored Terrorism in France:

One notable case of state-sponsored terrorism in France occurred in the 1980s, when the Libyan regime under Muammar Gaddafi provided support to militant groups targeting French interests. This support included training, funding, and arms supply. These actions culminated in the bombing of a French passenger airplane over Niger in 1989, resulting in the deaths of all 170 individuals onboard. This case highlights the extent to which state-sponsored terrorism can escalate and the challenges it poses for intelligence agencies in preventing such attacks.

Another case study focuses on the role of state-sponsored cyberterrorism in France. As a technologically advanced society, France has been a target of cyberattacks sponsored by state actors. These attacks aim to disrupt critical infrastructure, steal sensitive information, and create chaos in the digital realm. Understanding the methods and motivations behind state-sponsored cyberterrorism is crucial for developing effective countermeasures and enhancing international cooperation in combating this evolving threat.

Implications and Recommendations:

State-sponsored terrorism in France has significant implications for international diplomacy, nuclear proliferation, and proxy wars. It underscores the importance of intelligence agencies in gathering accurate information, analyzing threats, and formulating appropriate responses. Additionally, it highlights the need for increased cooperation among nations to combat state-sponsored terrorism effectively.

Conclusion:

The case study on state-sponsored terrorism in France sheds light on the various aspects of this complex phenomenon. By examining the motivations, tactics, and consequences of state-sponsored terrorism in France, scholars, academicians, and the general public can gain a deeper understanding of the challenges posed by this threat not only in Europe but also globally. Ultimately, this knowledge can contribute to the development of more effective strategies to mitigate the risks associated with state-sponsored terrorism and promote international security and stability.

Comparison of State-Sponsored Terrorism in Europe

State-sponsored terrorism is a complex and significant issue in today's global political landscape. This subchapter aims to provide an in-depth analysis and comparison of state-sponsored terrorism in Europe. By examining various case studies and current trends, this chapter seeks to shed light on the unique characteristics, challenges, and implications of state-sponsored terrorism in the European context.

One of the key aspects of state-sponsored terrorism in Europe is its historical roots. Unlike other regions, Europe has a long history of nationalistic and separatist movements, which have often resorted to terrorism as a means to achieve their political objectives. The subchapter will delve into the historical evolution of state-sponsored terrorism in Europe, highlighting prominent incidents and their impact on international relations.

The subchapter will also explore the different factors that contribute to state-sponsored terrorism in Europe. These factors range from political ideologies, ethnic and religious tensions, to the influence of external actors. By examining case studies such as the Irish Republican Army (IRA) in the United Kingdom, Basque separatist group ETA in Spain, and the Red Brigades in Italy, the subchapter will analyze the diverse motivations and strategies employed by state-sponsored terrorist organizations in Europe.

Furthermore, the subchapter will address the role of intelligence agencies in combating state-sponsored terrorism. It will examine the challenges faced by European intelligence agencies in gathering accurate and timely information, as well as the importance of international cooperation in intelligence sharing. The subchapter will also discuss the effectiveness of counterterrorism measures implemented by European states and the impact of these measures on civil liberties and human rights.

In addition, the subchapter will highlight the link between state-sponsored terrorism and international diplomacy. It will analyze how state sponsors of terrorism exploit diplomatic channels to support and protect terrorist organizations, as well as the diplomatic efforts undertaken by European states to counter state-sponsored terrorism.

Lastly, the subchapter will discuss the implications of state-sponsored terrorism in Europe for nuclear proliferation and proxy wars. It will examine how state sponsors of terrorism exploit regional conflicts to advance their own political and strategic interests, as well as the potential consequences for global security and stability.

Overall, this subchapter provides a comprehensive examination of state-sponsored terrorism in Europe, offering valuable insights for scholars, academicians, and the general public interested in the niches of states sponsoring terrorism, state-sponsored terrorism in the Middle East, Asia, Africa, Latin America, cyberterrorism, nuclear proliferation, proxy wars, international diplomacy, and the role of intelligence agencies. By understanding the unique characteristics and challenges of state-sponsored terrorism in Europe, policymakers and researchers can develop more effective strategies to combat this global threat.

Chapter 8: State-Sponsored Terrorism and Nuclear Proliferation

The Link between State-Sponsored Terrorism and Nuclear Proliferation

Introduction:

State-sponsored terrorism has emerged as one of the most challenging issues in contemporary international relations. This subchapter aims to explore the intricate link between state-sponsored terrorism and nuclear proliferation, shedding light on the dangerous consequences this nexus has on global security. By examining case studies from various regions, including the Middle East, Asia, Africa, Latin America, and Europe, we will delve into the complexities and potential implications of state-sponsored terrorism in relation to nuclear proliferation.

Understanding the Link:

The link between state-sponsored terrorism and nuclear proliferation is rooted in the strategic objectives of states sponsoring terrorism. These states often seek to project power, exert influence, and destabilize their adversaries through unconventional means. Nuclear weapons, possessing immense destructive capabilities, enable them to achieve these objectives more effectively. By providing support to non-state actors engaged in acts of terrorism, states sponsoring terrorism can indirectly access and exploit nuclear capabilities, thereby enhancing their leverage and threatening global security.

Case Studies:

Examining state-sponsored terrorism in different regions allows us to understand the diverse motives and strategies employed by states in pursuit of nuclear proliferation. In the Middle East, for instance, Iran's support for Hezbollah and its nuclear ambitions have raised concerns worldwide. Similarly, North Korea's notorious nuclear program and its alleged links with state-sponsored cyberterrorism highlight the dangerous nexus between terrorism and nuclear weapons.

Implications for Global Security:

The link between state-sponsored terrorism and nuclear proliferation poses significant challenges to international security. The potential acquisition of nuclear weapons by non-state actors supported by states sponsoring terrorism creates the risk of catastrophic terrorist attacks. Furthermore, the proliferation of nuclear weapons in volatile regions may trigger proxy wars and heighten tensions between states, leading to a potential nuclear arms race.

The Role of International Diplomacy and Intelligence Agencies:

Addressing the link between state-sponsored terrorism and nuclear proliferation requires robust international cooperation, diplomatic initiatives, and intelligence sharing. By engaging in dialogue and negotiations, states can work towards non-proliferation agreements and disarmament treaties. Intelligence agencies play a crucial role in uncovering clandestine nuclear activities and identifying the illicit transfer of nuclear materials, thereby aiding international efforts to counter state-sponsored terrorism.

Conclusion:

Understanding the link between state-sponsored terrorism and nuclear proliferation is essential for scholars, academicians, and the general public to comprehend the complex dynamics of international relations. By examining case studies from various regions and considering the implications for global security, this subchapter sheds light on the urgent need for international cooperation, diplomacy, and intelligence sharing to mitigate the risks associated with this dangerous nexus. Only through collective efforts can we effectively address the challenges posed by state-sponsored terrorism and nuclear proliferation, ensuring a safer and more secure world.

Case Study: State-Sponsored Terrorism and Iran's Nuclear Program

Introduction:

In this subchapter, we delve into a case study that sheds light on the complex relationship between state-sponsored terrorism and Iran's nuclear program. This case study offers valuable insights into the intersections of state-sponsored terrorism, international diplomacy, intelligence agencies, and the grave issue of nuclear proliferation. By examining this specific case, scholars, academicians, and the general public can gain a deeper understanding of the challenges posed by state-sponsored terrorism and its implications on global security.

Background:

Iran has long been accused of engaging in state-sponsored terrorism, with numerous incidents attributed to its proxies and intelligence agencies. Simultaneously, the country has pursued an ambitious nuclear program, raising concerns among the international community about its intentions and the potential for nuclear proliferation in the region. This case study explores the intricate dynamics between state-sponsored terrorism and Iran's nuclear ambitions.

Key Findings:

1. State-sponsored terrorism and proxy wars: The case study reveals how Iran has effectively utilized proxy groups, such as Hezbollah in Lebanon, to advance its political agenda and exert influence in the Middle East. These groups have been involved in numerous acts of terrorism, further destabilizing the region.

2. State-sponsored terrorism and international diplomacy: The case study highlights the challenges faced by the international community in dealing with state-sponsored terrorism while engaging diplomatically with Iran. Balancing the need for negotiations and diplomatic solutions with holding perpetrators accountable for acts of terrorism poses a significant dilemma.

3. State-sponsored terrorism and nuclear proliferation: The case study examines Iran's nuclear program and the concerns it raises regarding nuclear proliferation. It explores the potential risks of a state engaged in terrorism acquiring nuclear weapons, further escalating regional tensions and threatening global security.

4. State-sponsored terrorism and the role of intelligence agencies: The case study emphasizes the critical role of intelligence agencies in uncovering and countering state-sponsored terrorism. It highlights the importance of intelligence sharing and collaboration among nations to effectively address this complex issue.

Conclusion:

This case study provides a comprehensive analysis of the intricate connections between state-sponsored terrorism and Iran's nuclear program. It serves as a valuable resource for scholars, academicians, and the public interested in understanding the multifaceted challenges posed by state-sponsored terrorism and its impact on international relations. By examining this case, we can gain insights into the role of intelligence agencies, the complexities of international diplomacy, and the urgent need for collective efforts to address state-sponsored terrorism and its potential for nuclear proliferation.

Case Study: State-Sponsored Terrorism and North Korea's Nuclear Program

Introduction

In this subchapter, we delve into the complex and ever-evolving issue of state-sponsored terrorism, focusing specifically on North Korea's nuclear program. By examining this case study, we aim to shed light on the intricate relationship between state sponsorship of terrorism and international relations. This chapter will be of great interest to scholars, academicians, and the public who are eager to understand the various facets of state-sponsored terrorism and its implications on global security.

North Korea's Nuclear Program: A Brief Overview

North Korea's nuclear program has been a cause for concern for the international community for several decades. The nation's pursuit of nuclear weapons has raised questions about the role of state-sponsored terrorism and its potential impact on regional stability. Scholars have extensively studied North Korea's nuclear program, analyzing its motivations, strategies, and the broader implications for international relations.

State-Sponsored Terrorism and North Korea

North Korea's involvement in state-sponsored terrorism has been a subject of debate and scrutiny. While the nation has been accused of engaging in various acts of terrorism, including the bombing of Korean Air Flight 858 in 1987, its direct involvement in acts of terrorism remains contested. However, evidence suggests that North Korea has provided support, including financial assistance and training, to terrorist organizations in the Middle East and Asia. This raises concerns about the nexus between state-sponsored terrorism and nuclear proliferation.

The Role of Intelligence Agencies and International Diplomacy

The case of North Korea's nuclear program highlights the critical roles played by intelligence agencies and international diplomacy in addressing state-sponsored terrorism. Intelligence agencies are tasked with gathering information about state-sponsored terrorist activities, monitoring nuclear proliferation, and assessing the potential threats posed by rogue nations. International diplomacy plays a vital role in negotiating non-proliferation agreements, imposing sanctions, and fostering diplomatic relations to curb state-sponsored terrorism.

Implications for Global Security

The nexus between state-sponsored terrorism and nuclear proliferation poses significant challenges to global security. The potential use of nuclear weapons by state-sponsored terrorist groups could lead to catastrophic consequences. It is, therefore, crucial for states sponsoring terrorism and the international community to work together to prevent the proliferation of nuclear weapons and combat state-sponsored terrorism effectively.

Conclusion

This case study on North Korea's nuclear program provides valuable insights into the intricate relationship between state-sponsored terrorism and international relations. By studying the motivations, strategies, and implications of state-sponsored terrorism, scholars, academicians, and the general public gain a deeper understanding of the complexities of this global challenge. The role of intelligence agencies, international diplomacy, and the potential consequences for global security highlight the urgent need for collaborative efforts to combat state-sponsored terrorism and prevent the proliferation of nuclear weapons.

International Efforts to Prevent State-Sponsored Terrorism and Nuclear Proliferation

State-sponsored terrorism and nuclear proliferation are two interconnected and grave challenges that threaten global security and stability. In recent years, the international community has become increasingly aware of the devastating consequences these phenomena can have and has consequently intensified its efforts to prevent and combat them. This subchapter explores the various initiatives and strategies employed by the international community to address state-sponsored terrorism and nuclear proliferation.

One of the key international efforts is the establishment of multilateral treaties and conventions aimed at preventing the proliferation of nuclear weapons. The Treaty on the Non-Proliferation of Nuclear Weapons (NPT) stands as the cornerstone of these efforts. It seeks to prevent the spread of nuclear weapons, promote disarmament, and facilitate the peaceful use of nuclear energy. The NPT has been ratified by the majority of states, and its implementation is overseen by the International Atomic Energy Agency (IAEA). The IAEA plays a crucial role in verifying states' compliance with their non-proliferation obligations and ensuring the peaceful nature of their nuclear programs.

Additionally, international organizations such as the United Nations (UN) and regional bodies like the European Union (EU), the African Union (AU), and the Association of Southeast Asian Nations (ASEAN) have been actively engaged in counter-terrorism efforts. These organizations collaborate on intelligence sharing, capacity building, and promoting dialogue among member states to address state-sponsored terrorism effectively. The UN Security Council has also adopted numerous resolutions targeting states that support terrorism, imposing sanctions and calling for international cooperation to prevent terrorist financing and recruitment.

Another significant aspect of international efforts is the role of intelligence agencies in gathering and sharing vital information on state-sponsored terrorism and nuclear proliferation. Intelligence agencies from different countries collaborate through intelligence-sharing networks, such as the Five Eyes (USA, UK, Canada, Australia, and New Zealand), to exchange information and coordinate efforts to counter state-sponsored terrorism and nuclear threats. These alliances enable nations to pool their resources, expertise, and technological capabilities to identify and disrupt potential terrorist activities and nuclear proliferation networks.

Furthermore, diplomatic efforts and negotiations play a crucial role in addressing state-sponsored terrorism and nuclear proliferation. Diplomatic channels provide an avenue for states to engage in dialogue, resolve conflicts, and address the underlying causes that contribute to state sponsorship of terrorism. Diplomatic initiatives, such as peace talks, can help de-escalate tensions and foster cooperation among states, reducing the incentives for resorting to state-sponsored terrorism or pursuing nuclear weapons.

In conclusion, international efforts to prevent state-sponsored terrorism and nuclear proliferation have become increasingly robust and coordinated. The establishment of multilateral treaties, collaboration among international organizations, intelligence sharing, and diplomatic negotiations all contribute to addressing these complex challenges. However, there is still much work to be done. Scholars, academicians, and the public must continue their engagement and support these efforts to ensure a safer and more secure world.

Chapter 9: State-Sponsored Terrorism and Proxy Wars

Understanding Proxy Wars and State-Sponsored Terrorism

Proxy wars and state-sponsored terrorism have become significant issues in today's international relations. This subchapter aims to provide a comprehensive understanding of these phenomena, shedding light on their causes, consequences, and implications for global security.

States Sponsoring Terrorism:

One aspect explored in this subchapter is the identification and analysis of states that sponsor terrorism. It delves into the motivations behind state sponsorship, such as political, ideological, or strategic considerations. The subchapter also examines the methods used by these states to support terrorist groups, including financial, logistical, and ideological assistance.

State-sponsored Terrorism in the Middle East, Asia, Africa, Latin America, and Europe:

This subchapter further examines state-sponsored terrorism in different regions across the globe. It explores the unique dynamics and regional factors that contribute to the prevalence of state sponsorship of terrorism in each area. By analyzing case studies and historical examples, it provides a nuanced understanding of the complex relationships between states and terrorist groups in these regions.

State-sponsored Cyberterrorism:

The subchapter also delves into the emerging issue of state-sponsored cyberterrorism. It explores the tactics, strategies, and motivations behind states' use of cyber attacks to further their political agendas.

The impact of cyberterrorism on international diplomacy and the role of intelligence agencies in addressing this growing threat are also discussed.

State-sponsored Terrorism and Nuclear Proliferation:

This section provides an in-depth analysis of the nexus between state-sponsored terrorism and nuclear proliferation. It explores how states that sponsor terrorism may seek to acquire or support the acquisition of nuclear weapons by terrorist groups. The subchapter examines the potential consequences and challenges posed by such scenarios, emphasizing the need for robust international cooperation to address this threat.

State-sponsored Terrorism and Proxy Wars:

Another important aspect covered in this subchapter is the relationship between state-sponsored terrorism and proxy wars. It unravels how states utilize proxy groups to achieve their strategic objectives, often blurring the lines between state-sponsored terrorism and conventional warfare. The subchapter explores the consequences of these proxy wars for regional stability and international security.

State-sponsored Terrorism and International Diplomacy:

Lastly, this subchapter delves into the role of international diplomacy in addressing state-sponsored terrorism. It explores the challenges faced by the international community in condemning and deterring states that sponsor terrorism. The subchapter also highlights the importance of effective diplomatic strategies, multilateral cooperation, and international law in countering state-sponsored terrorism.

Overall, this subchapter serves as a comprehensive resource for scholars, academicians, and the public interested in understanding the complex dynamics of state-sponsored terrorism and its implications for international relations, regional stability, and global security.

Case Study: State-Sponsored Terrorism in the Syrian Civil War

Title: Case Study: State-Sponsored Terrorism in the Syrian Civil War

Introduction:

The Syrian Civil War, which began in 2011, has been marked by the emergence of state-sponsored terrorism. This subchapter delves into the complexities of state-sponsored terrorism in the Syrian context, exploring its causes, implications, and the role of international relations. By examining this case study, scholars, academicians, and the general public can gain deeper insights into the broader implications of state-sponsored terrorism.

Background:

The Syrian Civil War witnessed the involvement of various state actors, supporting different factions, and fueling the conflict through terrorism. This subchapter unravels the intricate web of state-sponsored terrorism in the Middle East, providing an in-depth analysis of the complex relationships among states, non-state actors, and terrorist organizations.

State-Sponsored Terrorism in Syria:

The subchapter investigates the role of different states in sponsoring terrorism in Syria, including those from the Middle East, Asia, Africa, Europe, and Latin America. It explores the motivations behind such support, whether driven by strategic interests, ideological affiliations, or regional power dynamics.

Proxy Wars and State-Sponsored Terrorism:

The Syrian Civil War has served as a proxy battleground for regional and global powers. This subchapter examines how state-sponsored terrorism has been used as a tool in proxy wars, where states indirectly engage in conflicts by supporting terrorist groups aligned with their interests.

The Role of Intelligence Agencies and Diplomacy:

State-sponsored terrorism often involves intelligence agencies and diplomatic maneuvering. This subchapter explores the intricate relationship between intelligence agencies and state-sponsored terrorism, shedding light on the role of intelligence in facilitating or countering such activities. Additionally, it analyzes the impact of state-sponsored terrorism on international diplomacy and its implications for global security.

State-Sponsored Terrorism and Nuclear Proliferation:

The subchapter also investigates the potential nexus between state-sponsored terrorism and nuclear proliferation. It examines the risks associated with states supporting terrorist groups that may seek to acquire or use nuclear weapons, analyzing the challenges this presents to international non-proliferation efforts.

Conclusion:

This subchapter provides a comprehensive analysis of state-sponsored terrorism in the Syrian Civil War, addressing its implications for international relations, global security, and counterterrorism efforts. By understanding this case study, scholars, academicians, and the public can develop a nuanced perspective on the multifaceted nature of state-sponsored terrorism and its repercussions in various regions worldwide.

Case Study: State-Sponsored Terrorism in the Yemeni Civil War

Title: Case Study: State-Sponsored Terrorism in the Yemeni Civil War

Introduction:

The Yemeni Civil War has served as a tragic example of the devastating consequences of state-sponsored terrorism. This subchapter delves into the intricacies of this conflict, analyzing the various actors involved, their motivations, strategies, and the wider implications for international relations. By examining the Yemeni Civil War as a case study, we aim to shed light on the complex dynamics of state-sponsored terrorism and its profound impact on global diplomacy, intelligence agencies, and regional stability.

Understanding the Yemeni Civil War:

The Yemeni Civil War, which began in 2015, witnessed the involvement of multiple state-sponsored actors, most notably Iran and Saudi Arabia. These regional powerhouses saw the conflict as an opportunity to gain influence in the Middle East and further their own geopolitical agendas. Iran supported Houthi rebels, providing them with weaponry, funding, and training, while Saudi Arabia led a coalition backing the internationally recognized Yemeni government.

Proxy Wars and Terrorism:

The Yemeni Civil War also epitomizes the link between state-sponsored terrorism and proxy wars. By fueling the conflict through proxies, states can achieve their objectives without direct involvement. This subchapter will explore the role of state-sponsored terrorism as a means of waging proxy wars, with specific reference to the Yemeni context.

Impacts on International Diplomacy:

The Yemeni Civil War has significantly impacted international diplomacy, with states taking sides and forming alliances in response to the conflict. This subchapter will explore the diplomatic challenges faced by countries in the region and the wider international community, as they navigate the complexities of state-sponsored terrorism and its implications for regional stability.

Role of Intelligence Agencies:

Intelligence agencies play a critical role in combating state-sponsored terrorism. This subchapter will examine how intelligence agencies are involved in monitoring and countering state-sponsored terrorism, with a focus on the Yemeni Civil War. It will highlight the challenges faced by intelligence agencies in gathering accurate information, analyzing threats, and coordinating efforts with international partners.

Conclusion:

The case study of state-sponsored terrorism in the Yemeni Civil War serves as a compelling example of the complexities and far-reaching consequences of this phenomenon. By analyzing the motivations, strategies, and impacts on international relations, diplomacy, and intelligence agencies, this subchapter aims to deepen our understanding of state-sponsored terrorism and its role in shaping global dynamics. It provides valuable insights for scholars, academicians, and the public interested in state-sponsored terrorism, regional conflicts, and international relations.

Case Study: State-Sponsored Terrorism in the Ukrainian Crisis

The Ukrainian crisis that unfolded in 2014 brought to light the alarming issue of state-sponsored terrorism. This subchapter delves into the complex dynamics of the crisis and the role of state-sponsored terrorism in exacerbating the conflict. By understanding this case study, scholars, academicians, and the public can gain valuable insights into the broader realm of state-sponsored terrorism and its implications for international relations.

The Ukrainian crisis began when Russia annexed Crimea, a region historically and culturally tied to Ukraine. This act of aggression ignited a series of events that led to a full-blown conflict between pro-Russian separatists and the Ukrainian government. What has been largely overlooked in the mainstream discourse is the state-sponsored terrorism that played a significant role in fueling the conflict.

In this case, Russia stands accused of providing military support, training, and funding to the separatist groups in eastern Ukraine. These groups, often referred to as "rebels" in the media, carried out acts of violence, including bombings, assassinations, and kidnappings, targeting Ukrainian military personnel and civilians. Such acts, orchestrated and supported by the Russian state, qualify as state-sponsored terrorism.

The Ukrainian crisis is a stark example of how state-sponsored terrorism can manipulate and escalate conflicts. It demonstrates the significant role of external actors in supporting and facilitating terrorism as a means to achieve political objectives. This case study challenges the conventional understanding of terrorism as solely perpetrated by non-state actors.

Moreover, this case study highlights the regional implications of state-sponsored terrorism. As scholars and academicians delve into this subchapter, they will gain insights into the dynamics of state-sponsored terrorism in various regions. It sheds light on the different approaches, motivations, and consequences of state-sponsored terrorism in the Middle East, Asia, Africa, Latin America, and Europe.

Furthermore, this subchapter emphasizes the intersection of state-sponsored terrorism with other critical issues such as nuclear proliferation, proxy wars, international diplomacy, and the role of intelligence agencies. It prompts scholars and academicians to explore the complex relationships between these factors and state-sponsored terrorism, ultimately deepening our understanding of the challenges faced by the international community.

In conclusion, the Ukrainian crisis serves as a compelling case study to examine the intricate nature of state-sponsored terrorism. This subchapter provides scholars, academicians, and the public with valuable insights into the dynamics and implications of state-sponsored terrorism, fostering a more comprehensive understanding of this pressing issue. By analyzing this case study, we can better comprehend the role of state-sponsored terrorism in international relations and work towards effective strategies to counter and prevent such acts in the future.

Implications and Consequences of State-Sponsored Terrorism in Proxy Wars

State-sponsored terrorism has become a pervasive and pressing issue in international relations, with proxy wars being one of its most significant consequences. Proxy wars occur when a state supports and funds non-state actors to carry out acts of terrorism on its behalf, thereby allowing the sponsoring state to maintain plausible deniability. This subchapter explores the implications and consequences of state-sponsored terrorism in proxy wars, shedding light on its impact on various regions and aspects of global politics.

One of the primary implications of state-sponsored terrorism in proxy wars is the destabilization of the regions involved. States sponsoring terrorism exploit the existing political, ethnic, or religious fault lines in target countries, exacerbating conflicts and perpetuating violence. For instance, in the Middle East, state-sponsored terrorism has fueled the rise of extremist groups like ISIS, resulting in the displacement of millions and the collapse of state institutions. Similarly, in Asia, state-sponsored terrorism has contributed to the prolonged conflicts in regions such as Kashmir and Xinjiang, leading to regional tensions and hindering peace processes.

The consequences of state-sponsored terrorism in proxy wars extend beyond regional instability. State-sponsored cyberterrorism has emerged as a significant concern, as states utilize hacking, disinformation campaigns, and attacks on critical infrastructure to further their geopolitical objectives. This sophisticated form of state-sponsored terrorism poses a severe threat to national security and the global economy.

Furthermore, state-sponsored terrorism in proxy wars has implications for nuclear proliferation. Sponsoring states often seek to gain influence or deter adversaries, using terrorism as a tool. This can lead to a dangerous escalation of tensions, as seen in the case of North Korea and its support for terrorist activities. The proliferation of nuclear weapons raises the stakes and increases the potential for catastrophic consequences in proxy conflicts.

The role of intelligence agencies in combating state-sponsored terrorism cannot be understated. Effective international diplomacy and cooperation between intelligence agencies are essential in countering these threats. States sponsoring terrorism must be held accountable through diplomatic measures, economic sanctions, and international pressure.

In conclusion, state-sponsored terrorism in proxy wars has significant implications and consequences for global politics. It destabilizes regions, fuels radicalization, poses cyber threats, contributes to nuclear proliferation, and necessitates robust international cooperation. Scholars, academicians, and the public must recognize the intricate connections between state-sponsored terrorism, proxy wars, and international relations to foster informed discussions and develop effective strategies to address this pressing issue.

Chapter 10: State-Sponsored Terrorism and International Diplomacy

The Role of Diplomacy in Countering State-Sponsored Terrorism

Introduction:

State-sponsored terrorism poses a significant threat to global security and stability. This subchapter explores the crucial role of diplomacy in countering this dangerous phenomenon. Diplomatic efforts play a pivotal role in addressing the complex issues surrounding state-sponsored terrorism, as they involve negotiations, dialogue, and the building of international consensus. This subchapter aims to provide an in-depth analysis of the various aspects of diplomacy in countering state-sponsored terrorism, focusing on different regions and specific challenges.

States Sponsoring Terrorism:

The subchapter begins by shedding light on the states that sponsor terrorism, discussing their motivations and strategies. It examines the geopolitical, ideological, and economic factors that drive states to support terrorist organizations. Additionally, it explores the challenges faced by the international community in dealing with these states, emphasizing the need for diplomatic approaches to bring about change.

State-Sponsored Terrorism in Different Regions:

The subchapter then delves into the specific regions affected by state-sponsored terrorism. It examines the Middle East, Asia, Africa, Latin America, and Europe, highlighting the unique challenges each region faces. By analyzing case studies and diplomatic efforts in these regions, scholars and academicians can gain a comprehensive understanding of the diverse tactics used by states to sponsor terrorism and the diplomatic efforts required to counter them effectively.

State-Sponsored Cyberterrorism:

With the increasing reliance on technology, state-sponsored cyberterrorism has emerged as a potent tool for destabilization. This subchapter explores the role of diplomacy in addressing cyber threats and the need for international cooperation to develop norms and regulations. It also examines the challenges faced in attributing cyberattacks to specific states and the diplomatic approaches required to hold state-sponsors accountable.

State-Sponsored Terrorism and Nuclear Proliferation:

The subchapter further addresses the nexus between state-sponsored terrorism and nuclear proliferation. It discusses the risks associated with states providing support to terrorist organizations seeking access to nuclear weapons. Diplomatic efforts, such as non-proliferation treaties and negotiations, are crucial in countering this threat and ensuring that nuclear materials do not fall into the wrong hands.

State-Sponsored Terrorism and Proxy Wars:

Proxy wars, fueled by state-sponsored terrorism, create complex challenges for international diplomacy. This subchapter examines the interplay between state-sponsors, their proxies, and diplomatic efforts to mitigate the consequences. It emphasizes the importance of diplomatic negotiations to de-escalate conflicts and prevent further destabilization.

State-Sponsored Terrorism and Intelligence Agencies:

Lastly, the subchapter explores the role of intelligence agencies in countering state-sponsored terrorism. It highlights the importance of intelligence sharing, coordination, and cooperation among nations to effectively combat this threat. Diplomatic efforts in building trust and sharing crucial information are vital in preventing terrorist attacks and dismantling state-sponsored networks.

Conclusion:

In conclusion, this subchapter emphasizes the pivotal role of diplomacy in countering state-sponsored terrorism. By engaging in dialogue, negotiations, and international cooperation, nations can address the multifaceted challenges posed by state-sponsors. Scholars, academicians, and the wider public can gain valuable insights into the diplomatic strategies required to enhance global security and counter the menace of state-sponsored terrorism effectively.

Case Study: Diplomatic Efforts to Address State-Sponsored Terrorism in the Middle East

Chapter 5: Case Study: Diplomatic Efforts to Address State-Sponsored Terrorism in the Middle East

Introduction:

In this subchapter, we delve into the complexities of state-sponsored terrorism in the Middle East and the diplomatic dilemmas faced by international actors attempting to address this pressing issue. By examining specific case studies, we aim to provide scholars, academicians, and the public with a comprehensive understanding of the challenges faced in countering state-sponsored terrorism, the role of international diplomacy, and the involvement of intelligence agencies.

State-Sponsored Terrorism in the Middle East:

The Middle East has long been a hotbed for state-sponsored terrorism, with several countries using non-state actors to further their political agendas. This subchapter will investigate the various state actors involved, including Iran, Syria, and their proxies, such as Hezbollah and Hamas. We will analyze the motives behind state sponsorship and the impact it has on regional stability and security.

Diplomatic Efforts:

Addressing state-sponsored terrorism in the Middle East requires a sophisticated and multi-faceted approach. This chapter will explore the diplomatic efforts by international actors such as the United Nations, European Union, and regional organizations like the Arab League. We will examine the effectiveness of sanctions, diplomatic negotiations, and peace processes in curbing state sponsorship and promoting stability in the region.

Role of Intelligence Agencies:

Intelligence agencies play a crucial role in countering state-sponsored terrorism. This subchapter will shed light on the intelligence-sharing mechanisms employed by countries to gather information on state actors, their proxies, and their terrorist activities. We will also discuss the challenges faced by intelligence agencies in gathering reliable intelligence in politically volatile and secretive environments.

Case Studies:

Drawing from recent events, this subchapter will present case studies on state-sponsored terrorism in the Middle East. We will analyze the diplomatic efforts undertaken to address these challenges and the outcomes achieved. Case studies will include the Syrian Civil War, Iran's support for Hezbollah, and the Israeli-Palestinian conflict, among others.

Conclusion:

This subchapter provides a comprehensive analysis of the diplomatic dilemmas faced in countering state-sponsored terrorism in the Middle East. By understanding the intricacies of state sponsorship, the role of international diplomacy, and the involvement of intelligence agencies, scholars, academicians, and the public can gain insights into the complexities of this issue. Ultimately, this knowledge can contribute to the development of effective strategies to combat state-sponsored terrorism and promote peace and stability in the region.

Case Study: Diplomatic Efforts to Address State-Sponsored Terrorism in Asia

State-sponsored terrorism continues to pose a significant challenge to international relations, with its far reaching consequences impacting nations across the globe. One region that has been particularly affected by this menace is Asia, where several states have been implicated in supporting terrorism as a means to further their political agendas. In this chapter, we delve into the complexities and diplomatic dilemmas associated with addressing state-sponsored terrorism in Asia.

State-sponsored terrorism in Asia has taken various forms, ranging from the provision of financial and logistical support to extremist groups to the direct involvement of state actors in planning and carrying out acts of terrorism. This chapter examines prominent examples of state-sponsored terrorism in the region, such as Pakistan's alleged support for terrorist organizations targeting India and Afghanistan, and North Korea's involvement in cyberattacks against South Korea.

Efforts to address state-sponsored terrorism in Asia have required robust diplomatic strategies and collaborations. The international community has been actively engaged in condemning and pressuring states involved in sponsoring terrorism. Regional organizations, such as the Association of Southeast Asian Nations (ASEAN), have also played a crucial role in fostering dialogue and cooperation among member states to counter the threat.

One of the key challenges in addressing state-sponsored terrorism in Asia lies in the intricate web of alliances and proxy wars that often characterize the region. This chapter explores the complexities of navigating these dynamics and highlights the role of diplomacy in mitigating tensions and finding peaceful resolutions. It examines instances where diplomatic efforts have successfully yielded results, such as the negotiations between India and Pakistan following heightened tensions in the aftermath of terrorist attacks.

Furthermore, this chapter sheds light on the role of intelligence agencies in countering state-sponsored terrorism. The exchange of intelligence and collaboration among agencies from different countries have proven instrumental in uncovering and preventing terrorist activities. However, the challenges of information sharing and maintaining trust between nations remain significant obstacles that need to be addressed.

By analyzing the case study of state-sponsored terrorism in Asia, this chapter provides valuable insights for scholars, academicians, and the public interested in understanding the complexities surrounding this issue. It also contributes to the broader discourse on state-sponsored terrorism, its impact on international diplomacy, and the need for concerted efforts to address this global menace.

Challenges and Opportunities for International Diplomacy in Combating State-Sponsored Terrorism

State-sponsored terrorism continues to pose significant threats to global security and stability, making it imperative for the international community to address this issue through effective diplomacy. This subchapter explores the challenges and opportunities faced by international diplomacy in combating state-sponsored terrorism, with a focus on various regions and aspects of this complex problem.

In the Middle East, state-sponsored terrorism has been a persistent challenge, with countries like Iran and Syria supporting extremist groups that destabilize the region. Diplomatic efforts must prioritize the promotion of peaceful resolution to conflicts and encourage regional cooperation to address the root causes of terrorism.

Similarly, Asia has witnessed state-sponsored terrorism, particularly in countries like North Korea and Pakistan. Diplomacy must emphasize the need for these states to abandon their support for terrorist organizations and engage in dialogue to address their security concerns.

The rise of state-sponsored cyberterrorism presents a unique challenge to international diplomacy. Diplomatic efforts should focus on establishing norms and regulations to prevent cyberattacks and enhance cooperation between nations to counter this evolving threat.

In Africa, state-sponsored terrorism has had devastating consequences, with countries like Sudan and Libya supporting extremist groups. Diplomatic initiatives should prioritize capacity-building and cooperation with regional organizations to address the underlying causes of terrorism and promote stability.

Latin America has also experienced state-sponsored terrorism, with countries like Venezuela and Cuba supporting groups that threaten regional security. Diplomacy must encourage these states to cease their support for terrorism and engage in dialogue to address their grievances.

Europe has not been immune to state-sponsored terrorism, with Russia being accused of backing militant groups. Diplomatic efforts should focus on strengthening intelligence-sharing mechanisms and promoting cooperation to counter this threat effectively.

The nexus between state-sponsored terrorism and nuclear proliferation is another critical challenge. Diplomatic initiatives must prioritize non-proliferation efforts, strengthen international frameworks like the Non-Proliferation Treaty, and engage in constructive dialogues to prevent the misuse of nuclear technology by terrorist organizations.

Proxy wars fueled by state-sponsored terrorism pose additional challenges. Diplomacy must address the root causes of these conflicts, promote peace negotiations, and discourage states from using terrorist groups as proxies for their geopolitical interests.

International diplomacy has a crucial role to play in addressing state-sponsored terrorism. It should emphasize the need for increased intelligence cooperation, the sharing of best practices, and the adoption of coordinated strategies to combat this global menace.

Furthermore, intelligence agencies play a vital role in countering state-sponsored terrorism. Diplomatic efforts should promote enhanced cooperation between intelligence agencies, facilitate information sharing, and encourage the development of joint counterterrorism operations.

In conclusion, combating state-sponsored terrorism requires a multifaceted approach that prioritizes diplomacy, cooperation, and the addressing of root causes. International diplomacy must seize the opportunities presented by emerging global challenges to effectively combat state-sponsored terrorism and promote peace and security worldwide.

Chapter 11: State-Sponsored Terrorism and the Role of Intelligence Agencies

The Importance of Intelligence Agencies in Combating State-Sponsored Terrorism

State-sponsored terrorism has become an increasingly prevalent issue in today's complex global landscape. It poses significant challenges to international security and stability, affecting various regions such as the Middle East, Asia, Africa, Latin America, Europe, and beyond. As scholars, academicians, and the general public, it is crucial to understand the importance of intelligence agencies in combating this grave threat.

Intelligence agencies play a vital role in countering state-sponsored terrorism by collecting, analyzing, and disseminating critical information to relevant stakeholders. These agencies serve as the backbone of national security apparatus, providing valuable insights to governments, military forces, and law enforcement agencies. Their work is particularly essential in identifying and neutralizing terrorist networks operated and supported by state actors.

States sponsoring terrorism employ several tactics to achieve their objectives. These include funding, training, and equipping terrorists, providing safe havens, and even engaging in cyberterrorism. Intelligence agencies are at the forefront of monitoring and thwarting such activities. Through their surveillance capabilities, they can identify financial transactions, arms transfers, and communication networks used by state sponsors and their proxies.

The role of intelligence agencies is especially critical in regions like the Middle East, where state-sponsored terrorism is rampant. They gather intelligence on the complex web of relationships between state actors, terrorist organizations, and local militias. By understanding these dynamics, intelligence agencies can expose the state sponsors' involvement and their motives, allowing governments to take appropriate diplomatic and military actions.

Intelligence agencies also play a crucial role in preventing nuclear proliferation facilitated by state-sponsored terrorism. They closely monitor the acquisition and transportation of nuclear materials, as well as the activities of rogue states seeking to develop nuclear weapons. By detecting and disrupting such endeavors, intelligence agencies contribute significantly to global nonproliferation efforts.

Moreover, intelligence agencies help in countering state-sponsored terrorism by uncovering the linkages between terrorism and proxy wars. These agencies gather intelligence on the involvement of state actors in supporting armed groups in conflicts around the world. By identifying the flow of weapons, funding, and fighters, intelligence agencies can expose the role of state sponsors and work towards deescalating conflicts.

The importance of intelligence agencies in combating state-sponsored terrorism extends beyond their operational capabilities. They also contribute to international diplomacy by sharing intelligence with partner nations and participating in joint operations. The exchange of information and collaboration between intelligence agencies strengthens international cooperation in countering state-sponsored terrorism.

In conclusion, intelligence agencies play a pivotal role in combating state-sponsored terrorism. Their capabilities in collecting and analyzing information are crucial in identifying, exposing, and countering the activities of state sponsors and their proxies. As scholars, academicians, and the public, it is imperative to recognize the critical role intelligence agencies play in safeguarding international security and stability.

Case Study: Intelligence Agencies' Actions against State-Sponsored Terrorism in the United States

Introduction:

State-sponsored terrorism poses a significant threat to global security, and the United States has not been immune to its reach. This subchapter delves into a case study that analyzes the actions taken by intelligence agencies in the United States to counter state-sponsored terrorism. By focusing on this specific aspect, we can gain insights into the delicate balance between national security and international diplomacy. This case study also sheds light on the crucial role intelligence agencies play in identifying and disrupting state-sponsored terrorist activities.

Overview of the Case Study:

The case study examines multiple instances of state-sponsored terrorism in the United States, including those originating from the Middle East, Asia, Africa, Latin America, and Europe. It also explores the emerging threat of state-sponsored cyberterrorism and its potential impact on national security. Furthermore, the study explores the interconnectedness between state-sponsored terrorism, nuclear proliferation, and proxy wars, highlighting the complexities faced by intelligence agencies in addressing these multifaceted challenges.

Key Findings:

The case study reveals that intelligence agencies have played a crucial role in countering state-sponsored terrorism in the United States. By leveraging their expertise in intelligence gathering, analysis, and collaboration, these agencies have successfully identified and disrupted numerous terrorist plots. Their actions have not only prevented loss of life but have also safeguarded national security interests.

Moreover, the study underscores the importance of international diplomacy in addressing state-sponsored terrorism effectively. Intelligence agencies have worked closely with their global counterparts to gather intelligence, share information, and coordinate efforts to combat this pervasive threat. Such collaborations have proven instrumental in dismantling terrorist networks and holding state sponsors accountable.

Implications and Recommendations:

The findings of this case study have significant implications for scholars, academicians, and the public. They highlight the urgent need for increased research, analysis, and public awareness regarding state-sponsored terrorism. The study emphasizes the importance of strengthening international cooperation and intelligence sharing to effectively confront this global menace.

Furthermore, the case study underscores the critical role played by intelligence agencies in countering state-sponsored terrorism. It calls for continued support and resources to enhance their capabilities, including cutting-edge technology, training, and recruitment. Additionally, the study recommends the establishment of robust legal frameworks to enable intelligence agencies to operate within the boundaries of law while ensuring the protection of civil liberties.

Conclusion:

This case study provides a comprehensive understanding of the actions taken by intelligence agencies against state-sponsored terrorism in the United States. It highlights the multifaceted nature of this threat and underscores the importance of intelligence agencies in addressing it. By studying this case, scholars, academicians, and the general public can gain valuable insights into the complex dynamics of state-sponsored terrorism, its impact on international relations, and the role of intelligence agencies in maintaining global security.

Case Study: Intelligence Agencies' Actions against State-Sponsored Terrorism in the United Kingdom

Introduction:

State-sponsored terrorism has become a critical issue in international relations, posing significant challenges to global peace and security. This subchapter focuses on a case study that explores the actions undertaken by intelligence agencies in the United Kingdom to counter state-sponsored terrorism. It sheds light on the strategies employed by these agencies to safeguard national security and protect their citizens from the threats posed by state-sponsored terrorism.

Intelligence Agencies' Role:

Intelligence agencies play a crucial role in identifying and countering state-sponsored terrorism. In the United Kingdom, agencies such as MI5 and MI6 have been at the forefront of efforts to combat this menace. These agencies work tirelessly to gather intelligence, analyze threats, and disrupt terrorist activities, ensuring the safety and security of the nation.

Countering State-Sponsored Terrorism:

The intelligence agencies in the United Kingdom employ a range of tactics to counter state-sponsored terrorism. These include surveillance, infiltration of terrorist networks, intelligence-sharing with international partners, and collaboration with law enforcement agencies. By monitoring the activities of suspected terrorists and their state sponsors, these agencies have been able to prevent numerous attacks, dismantle networks, and bring perpetrators to justice.

Challenges Faced:

The fight against state-sponsored terrorism is not without its challenges. Intelligence agencies must navigate complex geopolitical dynamics, balance national security with international diplomacy, and adapt to rapidly evolving tactics used by terrorist organizations. Additionally, the rise of state-sponsored cyberterrorism has added a new dimension to the threat landscape, requiring intelligence agencies to enhance their capabilities in cybersecurity and technological intelligence gathering.

Lessons Learned:

The case study of intelligence agencies' actions against state-sponsored terrorism in the United Kingdom provides valuable insights for scholars, academicians, and the public. It highlights the importance of robust intelligence-gathering and sharing mechanisms, international cooperation, and the integration of technology in countering this global threat. The role of intelligence agencies in preventing nuclear proliferation, proxy wars, and maintaining international diplomacy is crucial in the fight against state-sponsored terrorism.

Conclusion:

State-sponsored terrorism poses a grave challenge to global peace and security. The actions of intelligence agencies in the United Kingdom serve as a model for other nations in countering this menace. Through their unwavering dedication, these agencies have successfully thwarted numerous terrorist plots and protected their citizens from harm. However, the fight against state-sponsored terrorism requires continued vigilance, collaboration, and adaptability to effectively address this complex issue. By understanding the strategies and challenges faced by intelligence agencies in countering state-sponsored terrorism, we can enhance our collective efforts to create a safer world.

Collaboration and Information Sharing among Intelligence Agencies in the Fight against State-Sponsored Terrorism

The fight against state-sponsored terrorism is a complex and multifaceted challenge that requires a comprehensive and coordinated approach. In order to effectively combat this threat, intelligence agencies from around the world must collaborate and share information to enhance their understanding of the tactics, strategies, and networks employed by state sponsors of terrorism.

This subchapter explores the critical role of collaboration and information sharing among intelligence agencies in the fight against state-sponsored terrorism. It delves into the challenges and opportunities presented by this collaboration and highlights the importance of international cooperation in addressing this global security concern.

Intelligence agencies play a pivotal role in gathering, analyzing, and disseminating information related to state-sponsored terrorism. By pooling their resources and expertise, these agencies can generate a more comprehensive and accurate understanding of the threats posed by state sponsors of terrorism. This collective knowledge can inform policy decisions, guide counterterrorism efforts, and enable the development of effective strategies to disrupt and dismantle terrorist networks.

Collaboration among intelligence agencies is particularly crucial in regions heavily affected by state-sponsored terrorism, such as the Middle East, Asia, Africa, Latin America, and Europe. By sharing information on emerging trends, recruitment strategies, financing mechanisms, and operational tactics, agencies can better anticipate and respond to evolving threats. This collaborative approach can also help identify common patterns and linkages between different state sponsors, facilitating targeted and coordinated counterterrorism efforts.

Moreover, with the rise of state-sponsored cyberterrorism, intelligence agencies must adapt and enhance their collaboration efforts to address this unique challenge. By sharing expertise in cybersecurity, intelligence agencies can better identify and mitigate cyber threats posed by state sponsors of terrorism. This collaboration can also assist in the development of robust cyber defense strategies, information sharing frameworks, and international norms to curb state-sponsored cyberterrorism.

Collaboration and information sharing among intelligence agencies are also critical in the context of nuclear proliferation and proxy wars. State-sponsored terrorism often intersects with these issues, amplifying the risks and complexities involved. By exchanging information on illicit nuclear activities, arms transfers, and proxy support, intelligence agencies can contribute to a more comprehensive understanding of the dynamics at play and work towards effective non-proliferation efforts.

In conclusion, collaboration and information sharing among intelligence agencies are vital in the fight against state-sponsored terrorism. Scholars, academicians, the public, and all those interested in international relations must recognize the significance of this cooperation and advocate for enhanced collaboration and information sharing between intelligence agencies worldwide. Only through collective action and a shared commitment to defeating state-sponsored terrorism can we hope to counter this grave threat to international peace and security effectively.

Conclusion: Addressing Diplomatic Dilemmas in State-Sponsored Terrorism

In this book, "Diplomatic Dilemmas: State-Sponsored Terrorism and International Relations," we have explored the complex and intricate world of state-sponsored terrorism and its implications on international diplomacy. Throughout the chapters, we have delved into the various facets of this phenomenon, examining its presence in different regions and its connection to nuclear proliferation, proxy wars, and cyberterrorism. We have also analyzed the role of intelligence agencies in countering state-sponsored terrorism.

Our findings have shed light on the gravity of state-sponsored terrorism and the urgency to address its challenges effectively. It is crucial to recognize that state-sponsored terrorism not only threatens the security of individual states but also jeopardizes global peace and stability. The consequences of this form of terrorism extend far beyond the countries directly involved, impacting the entire international community.

One of the key takeaways from our exploration is the need for a comprehensive and coordinated approach to tackle state-sponsored terrorism. This requires international collaboration, where scholars, academicians, and the public must actively engage in understanding and addressing this issue. States sponsoring terrorism, particularly those in the Middle East, Asia, Africa, Latin America, and Europe, need to be held accountable for their actions. It is imperative to develop a multilateral framework that condemns and discourages states from supporting terrorism, imposing strict sanctions, and promoting accountability through international law.

In addition, the role of intelligence agencies cannot be understated. These agencies play a crucial role in gathering information, analyzing threats, and sharing intelligence to prevent terrorist attacks. It is essential to enhance cooperation and information sharing among intelligence agencies globally to effectively counter state-sponsored terrorism.

Furthermore, the international community must recognize the connection between state-sponsored terrorism and proxy wars. By addressing the root causes of proxy conflicts and fostering diplomatic dialogue, a more stable environment can be created, undermining the support for state-sponsored terrorism.

Lastly, the threat of state-sponsored cyberterrorism cannot be ignored. As technology continues to advance, so do the capabilities of state-sponsored actors in cyberspace. Cooperation between nations in developing robust cybersecurity measures and sharing information is vital to mitigate the risks posed by such attacks.

Overall, the conclusion drawn from our analysis is that addressing diplomatic dilemmas in state-sponsored terrorism requires a multi-faceted approach that encompasses international cooperation, accountability, intelligence sharing, and targeted measures to counter cyberterrorism. Scholars, academicians, and the interested public must continue to study and engage in discussions surrounding this critical issue. By doing so, we can collectively strive towards a world free from the threats posed by state-sponsored terrorism and safeguard international peace and security.

References.

References

In this subchapter, we will explore the extensive references that have been made available to us regarding the complex and challenging topic of state-sponsored terrorism. These references are essential for scholars, academicians, and the public alike, providing a comprehensive understanding of the various dimensions and implications of this global issue.

States Sponsoring Terrorism:

1. Hoffman, B. (2006). Inside Terrorism. Columbia University Press.

2. Byman, D. (2014). Al Qaeda, the Islamic State, and the Global Jihadist Movement: What Everyone Needs to Know. Oxford University Press.

3. Pillar, P. R. (2001). Terrorism and US Foreign Policy. Brookings Institution Press.

State-sponsored terrorism in the Middle East:

1. Levitt, M. (2015). Hezbollah: The Global Footprint of Lebanon's Party of God. Georgetown University Press.

2. Byman, D. (2017). Road Warriors: Foreign Fighters in the Armies of Jihad. Oxford University Press.

3. Hafez, M. M. (2006). Suicide Bombers in Iraq: The Strategy and Ideology of Martyrdom. United States Institute of Peace Press.

State-sponsored terrorism in Asia:

1. Cronin, A. K. (2009). How Terrorism Ends: Understanding the Decline and Demise of Terrorist Campaigns. Princeton University Press.

2. Gupta, D. K. (2011). India's State-Sponsored Terrorism in South Asia. Pentagon Press.

State-sponsored cyberterrorism:

1. Libicki, M. C. (2009). Conquest in Cyberspace: National Security and Information Warfare. Cambridge University Press.

2. Denning, D. E. (2000). Information Warfare and Security. Addison-Wesley.

State-sponsored terrorism in Africa:

1. Pham, J. P. (2012). Somalia: State Collapse and the Threat of Terrorism. Oxford University Press.

2. Forest, J. J. F. (2013). Countering Terrorism and Insurgency in the 21st Century: International Perspectives. Praeger.

State-sponsored terrorism in Latin America:

1. Kirk, R. (2010). More Terrible Than Death: Massacres, Drugs, and America's War in Colombia. PublicAffairs.

2. Ronfeldt, D., Arquilla, J., & Zanini, M. (2011). Networks and Netwars: The Future of Terror, Crime, and Militancy. RAND Corporation.

State-sponsored terrorism in Europe:

1. Burleigh, M. (2017). The Best of Times, The Worst of Times: A History of Now. Penguin Books.

2. Jarvis, L., & Lister, M. (2015). Theories of Terrorism: An Introduction. Routledge.

State-sponsored terrorism and nuclear proliferation:

1. Sagan, S. D. (2017). The Limits of Safety: Organizations, Accidents, and Nuclear Weapons. Princeton University Press.

2. Albright, D., & Steinberg, S. R. (2010). Solving the North Korean Nuclear Puzzle. Columbia University Press.

State-sponsored terrorism and proxy wars:

1. Gause III, F. G. (2013). Saudi Arabia in the New Middle East: Council Special Report No. 63. Council on Foreign Relations.

2. Luttwak, E. N. (2013). Strategy: The Logic of War and Peace. Harvard University Press.

State-sponsored terrorism and international diplomacy:

1. Rosati, J. A., & Scott, J. M. (2018). The Politics of United States Foreign Policy. Cengage Learning.

2. Biersteker, T. J., & Eckert, S. E. (2012). Countering the Financing of Terrorism. Routledge.

State-sponsored terrorism and the role of intelligence agencies:

1. Pillar, P. R. (2011). Intelligence and U.S. Foreign Policy: Iraq, 9/11, and Misguided Reform. Columbia University Press.

2. Richelson, J. T. (2012). The US Intelligence Community. Westview Press.

These references provide a solid foundation for scholars, academicians, and the public to delve into the multifaceted aspects of state-sponsored terrorism. By consulting these sources, readers can gain a deeper understanding of the historical context, regional dynamics, and policy implications associated with this pressing global issue.

9 798822 365920